Cecile tells the story of how she overcame shame and loss of hope to discover and love the beauty of her mother's soul and mind. *Loving Her Mind* is a must read for families and friends of persons with mental illness.

—Xavier Amador,
Psychologist and Author of *I'm Not Sick, I Don't Need Help!*

Discover that you are not alone in your experience with caring for a person with mental illness. In *Loving Her Mind*, you will be enCOURAGED to tell your story instead of hiding it, reach out for help and break the stigma surrounding brain disease.

—Yousry Armanios, M.D. M.A.,
Addiction Specialist and Church Counselor

Cecile's sincerity and vulnerability are absolutely inspiring and encouraging. Her courageous account of her family's journey with mental illness is incredibly needed and I am grateful for it. *Loving Her Mind* is a book that I will be regularly giving to my patients' families.

—Mena Mirhom, MD,
Columbia University Medical Center

Bibawy masterfully and exquisitely retells a firsthand account of one of the most mysterious and misunderstood disorders in the field of psychology. *Loving Her Mind* is a must-read for anyone who desires to build empathy and understanding around coping with mental illness.

—Patrick McMunn,
Professor of Psychology

Loving Her Mind will help a family member or friend of a person with mental illness find hope and courage to tell their story and break down the stigma that prevents healing.

—Hossam Guirgis, MD,
Associate Professor of Psychiatry,
The Ohio State University Wexner Medical Center

Loving Her Mind offers an opening to the closed-off and shame-filled world of a person growing up with and caring for a parent with schizophrenia. The reader will find hope and healing in the face of stigma and shame through this powerful, vulnerable story.

—Andrea Dalton,
Music Therapist,
Trauma Informed Care Consultant,
and Stephen Leader

This is a vulnerable and authentic account of a personal lived experience, written with beautiful honesty. Anybody living through a similar situation would take great comfort from reading it and knowing they are not alone.

—Marianne Mikhail,
MSc., Lead Counselor,
5th Avenue Counselling

Loving Her Mind offers a way to open the door to healing when shame is removed. Here, the reader will find hope for the loved ones.

—Char Aukland,
Owner of Whole Story Health Coaching

Loving Her Mind

Piecing Together the Shards of Hope

BY CECILE BIBAWY

Loving Her Mind Copyright © 2020 Cecile Bibawy
Printed in the United States of America
Published by Author Academy Elite
P.O. Box 43, Powell, OH 43035

All rights reserved. No part of this publication may be reproduced, stored
in a retrieval system, or transmitted in any form or by any means—for
example, electronic, photocopy, recording—without the prior written
permission of the publisher. The only exception is brief quotations in
printed reviews. adctd2house@yahoo.com website cecilebibawy.com

Paperback: 978-1-64746-498-1
Hardback: 978-1-64746-499-8
Ebook: 978-1-64746-500-1

Library of Congress Control Number: 2020917506

Scripture taken from the New King James Version®. Copyright © 1982
by Thomas Nelson. Used by permission. All rights reserved.

Dedication

To Mom, whom I love, after all.

Table of Contents

Part 1: Symptoms

Part 4: Stir Up Love

Foreword

One of God's blessings which we may forget to be grateful for is *sanity*. Most of us take our mental health for granted until we meet one day with someone, a spouse, a parent, a child, or an adult, who has a family member suffering from something like major depression or psychosis. With some mental conditions, it seems like the family member suffers much more than the patients themselves! During my clinical experience as a family physician and as a mental health counselor, I have come up with a serious conclusion: Mental illness affecting a family member can be the most devastating condition from which all other members suffer.

We may believe that when a patient is diagnosed with a mental illness by a mental health professional, pharmacological treatment or psychotherapy will put that condition under control. We may even assume that such patients, like most other patients, will follow their doctor's instructions by regularly taking their medications or by attending their therapy sessions. In real life, however, we generally see mentally-ill patients carrying high levels of resistance and low levels of compliance to treatment, adding more burdens to their family members.

In her book, Mrs. Cecile Bibawy, who lived that painful experience for very long years, portrays an impressively real picture of those families and how life in such a family setting reflects a bittersweet mix in which each individual must meet the daily challenges of living with a mentally-compromised member under the same roof. Reading this book will touch the bottom of any heart as it reveals how many families and children in our communities are struggling because a very significant other suffers from some sort of mental illness.

When you read this book, I am sure you will appreciate *sanity*, and you will begin giving thanks every morning for the blessing that we have taken for granted!

—Dr. Yousry Armanios, M.D. M.A.,
Addiction Specialist and Church Counselor

Note to the Reader

While this is my story, it is also my mother's. I've taken it upon myself to sort of blend two accounts into one, because in a way, they are inseparable of this story about living with Mom. I find that I *must* tell her story. I speak for her because she can't. If I don't speak up, how will others know they're not alone in the world of mental disease? How will they know what we did, how we coped, what worked, and what didn't?

I join the many others who have offered their experience. Hearing the stories is a way to get some hope. How can we keep hope alive? By keeping the lines of communication open and closing the doors of shame. By stirring up love that conquers fear and stigma.

Some names and identifying details have been changed.

I am grateful for the support of numerous friends and family members, without whom this work would not have been completed. Dana, Fr. Pishoy, Crystal, Michelle, and Meriam, you helped me in the early stages. April Giauque, for your outstanding insight and for helping me bring my story into the light the way my soul yearned to tell it. Alex, for all the talks and drinks at all the restaurants. Thanks for being the memory and reality that informed some of the indispensable parts of our story. I know it was not always easy to talk, but for me, that is what you did. Children, my morning glories, Juliana, Anastasia, Gabriel, and Amelia, for your patience when this project devoured my time and thoughts. Thank you for enjoying the process right along with me and for wanting the story to be told as much as I did. When I look at you and the more I know you, the more I see God's love, mercy, and hope. Anastasia, for the original painting that adorns the cover, sketched by your creative hands. George, my safe harbor, for seeing the book inside me before I did and for your undying, self-denying love. What did I do to deserve you? Nothing.

Above all, the Author of Love, my Savior and Lord Jesus Christ, who has brought me to this hour in peace, who gave me the words when I didn't have them, and who steered this project from the beginning.

Have you struggled with a mental illness? Are you a loved one or caregiver of a person who is struggling? If you are, I wish I could wrap my arms around you and tell you that you are loved, and not alone. Millions suffer with you. I suffer with you. I want you to know that even amid chaos, confusion, delusion, and despair, there is hope.

For You, Lord, are the helper of the helpless, the hope of the hopeless, and the Savior of the afflicted.
—St. Basil.

It's Time to Talk About It

When I was a student at The Ohio State University, I joined Makio, a student organization that annually published a yearbook to reflect undergraduate life. For three years, and even as production manager junior year, I enthusiastically delved into the stories of thousands of students, wrote them down, edited them, and remembered a few of them for a long time. I recorded the background, events, and rewarding moments that culminated in a volume of memories they wanted to keep. In their interviews, I learned their challenges, achievements, and dreams and scribbled them down on paper. I kept the notes for a while. I must have eventually thrown them away.

As a young journalism graduate, I continued to write people's stories for employers — testimonies of oral health patients, homeless people, and at-risk youth. Time passed, and I wrote about my husband, our kids, and the saints.

Then one day, I realized how little of my own life I had ever told. When the idea entered my mind to do so, I quickly pushed it away. Never had I written about my mother—my secret. I had been telling everyone's story except for the one I knew best and the one I had hidden the most.

Here's where this little tale takes a sharp turn, for I will now tell you mine.

PART 1

Symptoms

CHAPTER 1

Sheila

My First Lost Friend
1984

"What a pretty smile you have!" Mom sings as she opens the door for my friend to enter the house. My heart is beating fast. In my thirteen years, I don't remember having a friend spend the night. It's our first sleepover, and Sheila and I are best friends. At least that's what I tell myself. I love her to death. She is cute and fun and sweet. She is short like me, but most of all, we are friends. I am beyond excited as we watch a movie and share secrets. I tell her my secret crush, Joey Brickshaw. Somehow, I know she won't say anything. Sheila laughs easily and is shy like me. I know we will always be best friends.

A few days later, I waltz in the door from school and chatter about my day to Mom as she chops the onions for the string beans cooked in tomato sauce. She begins to fry them in Crisco shortening, and the house is about to fill with an aroma intoxicating to an empty stomach. Mom and I talk about this and that, then Sheila comes up. I mention our chats and plans for another sleepover.

"Oh, no, she's never coming here again," she states, eyes widening and grave. I am confused. The sinking of my heart begins now.

"What? Why not?"

"Didn't you see how she looked at me? She revealed herself to me. She knows me. We understand each other."

"What are you saying?" I ask with emotion. It feels like someone dropped a bowling ball on my stomach.

"What do you mean she revealed herself to you? It was a sleepover. She's my friend. You were laughing with us! I don't understand. This doesn't make any sense."

"She and her mother are evil, ya rohy (sweetheart). You can't speak to her ever again. She is not really your friend. She is my enemy. She was just using you to get to me."

"No ..." Sheila—using me?

"Then, why is she so nice to me? Why were you so nice to her?"

"I had to be!" Her voice rises a little.

"I don't want her to know that I know her. The less she knows, the better. The less dangerous she is. You must out-smart evil, but it's impossible to do that. Even for me, I can't do it because I am good. They are evil. Everything is an act. I know this is hard for you, but in school, you are to avoid her. Never speak to her. And, of course, she can never come to this house again."

Dangerous? Evil? What? This is not real.

"She is my best friend! She's not any of those things. She can't be! Please." My heart sinks deep. I finally have a best friend of my own, and she turns out to be evil? Is she just acting?

"She is so happy and nice. We shared secrets. I thought—"

"Don't share any more secrets with her," Mom interjects. "She will use them against you and me. Don't you care about me? I am your mother. You must trust me; I would not lie to you, you know. And since they are doing this to your mother, you must stay away from her and her family."

My brain is at war with my heart, which does not foresee its future hunger of longing for friendships that I can never have. Though this doesn't seem exactly right, it must be true. Mom wouldn't lie to me. It sounds bad. There is a sharp edge of urgency in her voice. I can't figure it out. She keeps talking about danger and evil. I don't feel unsafe around my friend and her mother.

I must do what Mom says. There are no other options. I must keep Mom and me and my little siblings safe. Sheila and I have one more conversation. The one in which I tell her that we are not friends anymore. I don't remember the exact words, but I remember there is yelling. Then, though we attend the same high school, I avoid her everywhere. I'm not going to let anyone use my mother or me. My loyalty is with my mother. I must be a good daughter.

Sheila and I never speak to each other again.

CHAPTER 2

On The Inside Looking Out

Lily's Early Life

I know little about my Mom's childhood. I wish I knew more. I wish there were more stories and more pictures. She was born Lily Makar in the 1940s in Cairo, Egypt, to Makar Tayeb Solimon and Therese Labib Mounir. She is the fourth in a line of eight children plus one who died before the age of three. Lily has two younger sisters and five brothers.

At seven or eight years, she saw her mother crying in the living room while nursing her little brother. No one was telling her the reason for the sadness and confusion in the house. She ran up to little Elham's room and found her lying flat in her crib, and her face covered with her blanket. She uncovered her face, and found a shell of the baby sister she had carried, and helped care for her entire sprouting life.

Seeing the tiny body, young Lily ran to her room, crying. Hearing her crying, her father followed his daughter to her room and asked her softly, "why are you crying?" and walked out—as nothing had happened. Mom said "*hush*" *was the word*. She said, "we did not speak about such things." No one spoke about Elham again. "You just didn't talk about it," she said.

Growing up, Mom and her family moved frequently. Wherever they landed, Mom attended the private school in the area. However, one town they lived in did not have a French school nearby. Public school was not feasible because she would not have understood Arabic. Mom stayed home for four years and helped her mother take care of the younger siblings.

Mom called it *miserable*. She hated staying home while her siblings went to school. When they finally moved again, they took up residence near a Catholic French immersion in Shoubra, a suburb of Cairo. Notre Dame Des Aportres largely influenced her cultural values. She adopted a Western mindset and a distinct affinity for the Catholic Church. Unlike her public-school counterparts, which included her siblings, she did not have to learn the Koran teachings. For her, Arabic was more of a second language than a first.

After immigration and marriage, she enrolled in the community college in New Jersey, where I was born. Her middle school diploma, written in French, passed as a high school diploma because they couldn't read it, procuring her entry. The college admissions people never knew the better, and Mom became a college student. The associate degree was the needed steppingstone on her path to university, which was her ultimate goal.

To her core, Mom is a fiercely independent woman. What was to happen to her would drastically deflate the fierceness and diffuse the potential power of any dreams she ever had.

CHAPTER 3

Trapped

Being Married

My parents immigrated separately to Canada, Dad alone, Mom with her family. By the late 1960s, very few Copts had immigrated to North America. The pool of Christian Egyptians was small, so pickings were slim. Introduced by the priest of St. Mark's Church in Toronto, Edward met Lily and asked the priest for her hand. Lily, who was not interested and told her father as much, was told by the priest and her parents that she should say yes. "He is a good man," said the priest. They were married in 1968.

My parents first lived in New Jersey, and from Mom's talk, the only thing she really liked about Camden, New Jersey, was her supersized kitchen. There was no family around, and she was a new immigrant, only having lived a few years in Canada prior to this stage. During that time in Camden, Mom told a story of a man with a camera, who snapped a picture of me while carrying me on a street corner. He took off without a word to her. She always said my photo must have been worth a lot of money and that she was cheated. By 1974, they landed in the friendly American Midwest. Ohio became their life.

Before she had children, Mom painted on canvas with oils. Her deft, slim hands sketched Nefertiti, Virgin Mary, and impressionistic landscapes. They charmed the viewer with deep shades and layers of color, texture, and feeling. She never took art lessons.

The depiction of the Virgin sparkled with a gold halo of glitter around her head. Her large, sad eyes, clear blue like the sky in May's morning, reminded you of her future sorrow over the Child Jesus, who sat on her lap. Mary wore a deep red gown with an ivory-toned robe draped around her. Her delicate head covering was white with lace trim. Her hair was chocolate brown, and her flawless face was white, tinted with a faint rose hue. Her red lips were closed. She was neither smiling nor frowning, only pondering. Her heart swelled with love. How did my mother draw love in only a face—all the love of the world's people in St. Mary's face.

The Child, with the same eyes as His mother, was one or two years old. His hair was light brown with short, tight curls. He was wearing a light blue tunic. He was smiling softly and peered at the viewer before Him. One hand was over the Virgin's, and the other, His right hand, was held up in the traditional iconic way with the thumb, index, and middle fingers upright and leaning toward each other. Small white flowers with red centers surrounded them as they eagerly huddled close. They looked like the blooms of the Red Heart hibiscus.

She painted because she was bored out of her mind in New Jersey. When children arrived, there was no time to paint. Her works ornamented the walls of our house until we all moved out. Sometime after Dad died, she removed the painting of the Virgin off the wall of the upstairs hallway. She repeatedly scoffed when I swooned over her work. "They were not very good," she said. Years later, I found the piece in a plastic bag on the cement floor of the cobweb-laced, unfinished portion of the basement.

What was more tragic—that she was pressured into marrying a man against her will or stopped painting after I was born in 1971 and never picked up a paintbrush again?

She was a gifted artist. The fact that she passed it on to my sister Dalya and my daughter Anastasia was a redeeming relief and joy.

Art is a reflective expression of the mind and therapy. It heals the artist and the audience at once. It is a salve for the soul. I wished she had dusted off her palette and sketched even just a few more exquisite pieces for all our sakes.

Instead, she dove into motherhood with every ounce of her energy, effort, and wit. I, the first and only child for five years, came three years after marriage. Mom adorned me with black curls kept at chin length, pretty 70s-style dresses, and the traditional gold cross on a chain and gold studs for Sears portraits.

Dad was a professor in a podiatry school across the state border at the University of Pennsylvania. He loved to teach, and his students loved him. When he was offered a job at Chemical Abstracts Service in Columbus, his teaching career ended, but he always said it was teaching that he enjoyed the most.

He was very serious about his work, and his ethic was loftier than a giant redwood and stronger than a medieval keep. He had great respect for diligent people. His frequent migraines never tarnished his perfect attendance record. Somehow, he made it work, and he got to work. Once, when he received an award for perfect attendance, a co-worker queried, "What vitamins do you take?" I don't think he ever took vitamins.

My parents each stood five feet two inches tall, so Mom rarely wore high heels. She hated the fact that her husband was not taller than her. She fluctuated between compliance and defiance in the wearing of lipstick. He strongly disapproved of her wearing any loud makeup, especially bright or dark lip colors. Most of the time, when she went out, she wore a muted red, not too bold. He disallowed sleeveless tops, regarding them as immodest for Christian girls and women, even outside of church.

Because Dad never drank, alcoholic beverages were not to be found in our house. He occasionally consumed coffee and tea, avoided caffeine addiction, and on some evenings watched TV for entertainment. *Dallas* and *Falcon Crest* were their favorite evening diversions for a while.

Dad rarely deviated from his daily and weekly routines, including work, prayer, Bible reading, and other spiritual reading, followed by a short nap, then world news at 6:30 p.m. The weekend continued with Sunday morning liturgy, *60 Minutes* on Sunday evenings, and Billy Graham when his message was televised.

Over time, he mastered the art of saving money with coupons and frequented garage sales. He was an alien at the mall. Mom was its poster child. To describe him as frugal would understate it.

He didn't cook, clean, change diapers, dress children, or do yard work. As for Mom, a young immigrant, and a new mother, far away from her family, this was a devastating shock.

"I couldn't believe this was going to be my life. He wasn't going to do anything or say much of anything. I was overwhelmed with how alone I felt. I was completely miserable." she said.

He did not read fiction, wear cologne, go to the theatre or sports events, nor attend parties. He did not spend paid workdays for leisure, so we did not take vacations. Once, we accompanied Dad to a work conference in Florida and stayed with my uncle and his family. At eight years old, it was my first beach experience. I remember the smell of the warm, salty air breezing across my face and the strange-looking palm trees and thinking that I was in a different world altogether.

For his listening pleasure, Dad cranked up cassette-tape recordings of church hymns, spiritual sermons, and news radio. I don't remember him playing classical music, though, out of all the old composers, he always spoke most of his love for Tchaikovsky. Three of his famous works ranked in greatness in this order: *Swan Lake*, *Sleeping Beauty*, and *The Nutcracker*. Frequently, he tuned in to *Thru the Bible* with Dr. J. Vernon McGee, a weekly radio Bible study that aired every Saturday morning.

Mom always regarded Dad's lifestyle as excessively austere. She liked to buy things, and he did not. As much as he disapproved of her excessive spending habits, she perceived him missing out on life. The most unfortunate victims of this reality that left so much to be desired were her and the children.

I can't help but wonder if Gido and Teta, my grandparents, caught on to something before the marriage. Did they notice that something was off with their daughter? Did they discover an urgent need to secure a marriage before symptoms became apparent? Did they perceive Edward as her only option? Or the best option? I suppose we'll never know. She hated her harsh, humdrum life. In stark contrast, the life inside her mind, the life she believed she lived, screamed intrigue of dramatic proportions.

We're not sure where or how Mom picked up the term "psychopath." Back when I was little, she began to talk about the wiles of psychopaths. One was her sister's husband, a physician, and the first to emerge in her delusional talk. Perhaps the fact he was a doctor triggered her, or that he married the sister closest to her in age and proximity. In those days, the road trip to the nearest Coptic church was two and a half hours long. St. Mark's offered services every Sunday. We attended as often as possible, leaving early in the morning to catch the early Matins prayers. Dad drove the big red Buick as we slept in the back on the way home. Lily was doing all the talking.

"It doesn't matter that no one else knows. No one can tell except me. He is turning everyone in the family against me. He tricked Ferialle into marrying him. He is manipulating her and plays with her emotions," Lily said.

"How is he manipulating her?" Dad asked.

"Did you see how he looked at me? He was showing me that he knows me. He knows that I see evil and that I will understand who he is and what he is capable of. He is dangerous, Edward. We will never stay at their house again"

"What evil? What are you saying?" Dad asked in alarm.

"Abouna. My God, you have to tell him he has evil in his church. He must know. Will you tell him? That evil man is turning the whole church against me. I am not going back there again."

The next closest church would have been near Pittsburgh, four hours away. But Dad was not yet ready to give up.

"Boulos didn't do anything to you. He is a good man, helps people; he loves the church."

"Lies!" she interjected. "He wants you to believe that. Don't be a fool like everyone else. I know the truth! Even Ferialle treats me differently now. He flaunts his money and makes her wear more expensive clothes. He knows it will make us look worse. You married a very perceptive woman, Edward. I know things that no one else knows."

"What are you saying?" He would correct her thoughts right now. "None of this is true. I don't want you to say these things again, okay?"

"You can't see what I see!" The tension in her voice was rising. The same speech was delivered several more times while Dad mutely drove past tiny Ohio towns. After a short reprieve, she began the argument again.

He pulled over, silently stepped out of the car, and briskly walked to the guardrail and sat on it, gripping the sunlight with his eyes. The vehicles on the six-lane interstate sped by. They didn't stop to help him fix her mind. They just carried on to their destinations while normal life for this five-person family skidded to a screeching halt.

For the moment, sitting on the side of the highway in the afternoon air, he was under the sky, not trapped inside the car and inside her head. Now, his wife was alarmed. "Okay, okay, get back in the car," she pleaded tentatively. She had followed him to the rail.

"Never mind. Let's just keep going," she said.

In a few years, Dad will learn that the incessant rants were the manifestations of fixed delusions that would become a part of Lily, forever.

CHAPTER 4

I Wish We Were Normal

More Lost Friends
1984

Taking showers and using the toilet is weird. I have already struggled to keep a positive self-image, but knowing my body is perpetually on display before the unseen faces of a group of physicians from *The Ohio State University* is highly unsettling. Mom says they are observing us through a bug that has been inserted somewhere in the house. We are under surveillance.

Why are they watching me? I understand why they would need to study Mom. But why me? I'm an unimportant person who goes to school and then goes home. I'm just a normal kid.

I repeat the last statement, perpetually. But I might as well be a tawny frogmouth telling herself she's an owl. We are anything but typical. I fantasize about the privilege of being normal. The idea of it is a wisp of warm air whizzing past my face.

The tawny frogmouth is commonly mistaken for the owl. The bird has a strange-looking mouth and legs and is the weakest flier in the frogmouth genus. Their brown and gray colors blend with tree branches, so they go unnoticed. Their call sounds resemble grunts rather than the hollow woos of the illustrious owl.[1] This was me—strange, weak, and unnoticed. I deeply longed to be more like the owl.

Slivers of normal life slide in and out of the small windows of our olive-green colonial house with black shutters like afternoon sun rays. She lays dishes of delicious food on the table, and commands us to eat, like any proper Egyptian maternal authority. When I lie in bed in pain from menstrual cramps, she enters my room with brows furrowed and silently lays a picture of Pope Kyrillos VI on my nightstand. When I get a cold, the worried look on her face and thorough inspection of my symptoms soothe me as much as her chicken soup. When she remembers to check on me, she places a swift, soft, and slender hand on my forehead, looking for a fever. It is normal—a mother worried about her sick child.

In a memory barely there, she holds my hand with light, bony fingers. Her grip is firm enough to keep me attached to her. I am three years old, and I am prone to do this. This is my earliest and one of my scarcest memories of physical contact with her.

I am starved for ordinary interactions. I hear faint whispers of normal when she asks me about my day at school. But that particular normal lasts all of three minutes.

"What did you and your friends talk about in school today?" she asks, all ears. We're sitting on the red velvet couch in the family room. She turns off the TV and waits fixedly with her brown eyes.

"I didn't really talk to anyone today." My reserved self is lost in the halls throughout high school. Ninth grade was bearable. The tenth grade was okay. I had tried out for the cheerleading squad and did not make the cut. So, I decided on soccer and warmed the bench for two years. The coaches did not pay much attention to me. I don't remember hanging out with anyone on the team outside of practices and games.

Because competitive sports prove not to be my thing, I set my sights on music. Following a love for Broadway, I audition for a part in the Spring musical two years in a row, where all my hopes lay. I am cut both times. Stiff competition. Playing the piano, my only real skill is not an option either. Though I have been taking private lessons since I was nine years old, the only opportunity to play in high school is in the jazz band, but Mike Holmes, who is in my grade, holds a monopoly on that. He plays like Peanuts' Shroeder. I don't have a chance.

My school has a choir, which I take as an elective. The upperclassmen can audition for Concert Choir and sing on tour. For senior year, I audition and *make* the cut. My excitement soars to new heights. I am talented and accomplished, and I'm going places.

The first day after the list of concert singers is posted, the floor might as well be a cloud as I walk into the choir hall. While heading toward my chair, Mrs. Mokser calls me down to the piano.

"You didn't actually make it," she titters. "Your name wasn't supposed to be on the list. It was a mistake." She is shaking her head wistfully. I stare at her, unable to speak. I don't know what my face says, but she finishes her speech, indifferently, "You can stay in." Her smile is half; the crushing blow to me is whole.

Earlier in the year, I have a one-time, ten-minute limelight experience. The school holds a talent show in the gym every year. Once again, I audition before a panel of two. This time, I am given a spot in the program. Before the entire school and faculty, I play Richard Clayderman's arrangement of Ballade Pour Adeline. Hearing the roar of cheering and clapping when I finish my piece produces a giddy exhilaration that I have never felt. The piano is my superpower in high school.

"Why not?" Mom quizzes.

"I don't know," I reply.

Thinking about it, I am sure I talk to people—short conversations in the hallways, complaining about the teachers. I hang out with a group of girls in the first two years, but junior and senior high, I don't remember any friends at school. I think I don't know how to be a friend. How many teens do? I am pathetically awkward and cannot relax around people.

"No one talked to you—even at lunch? How come?" she presses.

"I don't know; I'm always in a hurry to get to my classes." Should we broach this again, or are we better off avoiding the subject of lunch? I hate lunchtime at school. I want badly to vomit my day on the kitchen table and have her put her arms around me. High school is a very cold place.

"Mom, no one talked to me again at lunch." I'm going to give this one last try. "And if they do say anything to me, it's mean, like 'Go to hell,' or they make fun of everything I say. I sit on the end at the table, and they pretty much ignore me the entire crappy time. Jenny Morgan is so ugly to me. She hates me! I don't even know why. I didn't do anything."

"No, you didn't do anything. It has nothing to do with you. They must have found out who you are."

"Mom …" I close my eyes and breathe deeply, slowly.

18

"You have to listen to me. I know what I'm talking about. How can you know? You can't see evil. Only I can, so you just have to believe me!" Her voice is rising again.

"Believe what? That all these girls are taking orders from a secret committee of psychiatrists from OSU? That we're being watched 24 hours a day, seven days a week? That I can't take a shower without eyes on me?"

"Just forget about that," she says in a half-whisper. "And don't say anything about that to your friends."

"I don't want to hear this." Again. I have heard it dozens of times.

"Did you tell them?" she asks heatedly.

"No!" I exclaim. She eyes me suspiciously.

"Well, why do you think they won't speak to you? What did you do wrong?" There is caution in her tone.

"Nothing, they just don't like me."

"Of course, you didn't do anything! It's not you. They are studying me. They're studying us. I am your mother. I know the truth. I am the only one that knows. You must know too, so they can't hurt you anymore. And you know what? They are trying to turn you against me —just like Boulos did! That evil turned the whole church against me. Do you want them to succeed?"

"No, of course not," I whimper. My insides are knotting. I'm trapped.

Uncle Boulos and Tante Ferialle and their kids, Nevine and Pete, have become estranged to us. I know from pictures that we hung out as little kids. My siblings, Mark and Dalya, five and six years younger than me, will have no memory of that time. I will not see or speak to anyone in this family till late high school. The first time I will see my cousins again will be at their church in Cleveland. Mom warns me all the time that Uncle Boulos might show up at any minute to kill Mark. From far away, he is a very scary man. We are forced to stay away from him and his family for more than a decade, during which Laila (her family nickname) and Ferialle have no contact.

"Well, they will if you don't believe me and if you don't do what I tell you," she says; her eyes have narrowed. I look away.

"Do what?" I ask feebly. I already know the answer.

"Don't talk to them. Leave them alone. I'd rather you don't have friends then have evil friends. Jesus is your friend. And I'm your friend. That's all you need."

In ninth grade, an incident will have me believing I will never have friends. When Mom stops at the gas station to fill the car, we are in the middle of a similar discussion about the girls at school, but we are arguing. I am trying to convince her that my friends really like me and are not just pawns in an evil scheme against her.

"Then I'll just drop you here," she said calmly.

"What? No!" I said.

"If you want to see them so badly, then they will come and get you."

"No, I don't have any plans with them now. Please, just let me come home!"

"I know they will come and get you, Ceci. Get out," she says. She is unhesitating.

"How? No one is coming! I promise—I'm not lying!" I plead.

"They told me. Now, get out!"

I step out of the car and watch her drive away with my little siblings in the back seat. The gas station attendant allows me to use the phone to call an older girl I know from school who drives—a junior. She picks me up and takes me straight home.

The end of my rope is beginning to come into view. I am getting sick of this—of trying to change her mind. But it is always worth another try, I reason. You just never know. One of these days, with my help, clarity might triumph over delusion.

But even if it never does, the secret about the psychiatrist is safe with me, because that's just too weird to tell anybody.

CHAPTER 5

Strained Relationships

When Dad Moved Out
1984

By the eighth grade, Mom and Dad are frequently fighting. The subject of their verbal scuffles toggles between how Mom spent the money and Dad's unwillingness to do something about the treacherous "psychopaths" in our lives.

Over and over, Mom loudly calls him unsupportive, unwilling to listen, stubborn, emotionless, and uncaring for her and the children. He is putting his family at risk for not calling the police when she told him to. She has to protect us, so he had to go. He sustains relationships with psychopaths. The fact they are his friends or family members does not matter. Though she reveals to him the truth about them, he won't believe her, so he has no place here. We are better off without him.

Dad, however, won't leave. For him, there is no divorce. You stay married because God is the One that brought you together, and He forbids divorce, as taught by the Bible and the church.

Later, when the older version of myself raises this point toward the question of his loyalty, Mom will claim that the only reason he did not want to leave is that he just wanted someone to cook his meals, wash his clothes, and fulfill his sexual needs. She harps unceasingly. Daily, she tells him they are going to separate. He is no longer allowed to stay there. If he can't act like a husband, then he can no longer be hers.

I don't remember his verbal responses. He explains later that he always answered definitively in the negative—sometimes gently, other times firmly.

"You're my wife. I can't leave you," he says.

But one day on the phone with my grandmother, Mom's mom, she asks Dad, "Is she really insisting you leave?"

"Yes," he says.

"Then go," she says, urgingly.

Teta Therese is the only person in my mother's family he trusts. He esteems her highly and respects her deeply. Everyone does—even her eight children, the spouses, and the grandchildren who are old enough to remember adoring her. Friends of the family call her a saint. He agrees to leave only when she finally gives the green light.

Dad moves into an apartment around the corner from the office. The complex is also near the university, so most of the residents are college students. He lives there for five years, four of them alone. During the fifth and final year, ten-year-old Mark, and I, at sixteen, will move in with him. Before that, I don't remember seeing him very often. Mom does not let him come to the house.

Though we are regular churchgoers, Mom stops attending our church when Dad moves out. He continues to go to the Coptic Orthodox church while Mom takes us to the Catholic. I am confirmed in the Catholic church in the eighth grade to seal our membership and the lower tuition for the affiliate school. Public school is not an option.

This year, I somehow end up in the principal's office. Sister Catherine and I are discussing my home life. She asks me a few questions and calmly points out some simple solutions.

I don't remember all the issues I raised or most of the conversation, but I look down a lot. I feel dirty, as I complain about our family dinner habits. Thought, *will she laugh at me? How much does she know about our problems? What does she think about our family? Does she know about Mom? Is she uncomfortable with us? Is she kicking me out of middle school?*

"My dad is always watching the news, even during dinner," I grumble. "We're not allowed to talk when it's on, and he blasts it. The news is the most important thing."

While local news is optional, Dad religiously watches the world news every night. He toggles among the three primetime stations to get it all. He explains to me when I'm older that the reason he never misses the news is that it is more reliable than Egypt's broadcasts, which he describes as completely corrupt. You can't believe anything on any channel there. At least here, you can get an idea of what the leaders are doing and what is going on in the world. (I wonder what he would say now about our media).

"Maybe you can eat dinner after the news," she suggests as if I have a say in the matter.

The meeting with the nun is perhaps an assessment or a counseling session, but all I want her to do is assure me that it is going to be okay and that it isn't my fault, that I have done nothing wrong. I wish she would drape her arm around me and hold me for a little while. But I am sitting across from her on the other side of her large desk. That would be a long reach.

Before I come to understand anything, Dad is my problem.

He is my problem because he is a problem for Mom. By now, I have absorbed every one of her grievances, which she voices incessantly. He is too quiet, emotionless, and lazy. He did not want children. The church is more important to him than his own family. He will not allow her to visit her parents in Canada as often as she desires, and he is stingy. She is never allowed to buy anything. Her monthly allowance is barely enough for food. He is always saying we don't have enough for her to buy what she wants, including pricey Nike shoes for Mark and trendy clothes for my sister and me.

Dad limits Mom's purchases. We are on a tight budget, so I don't get everything I want. I am always asking for new piano music, cassette tapes of my favorite pop artists and cosmetics. My request for new clothes is less frequent because I wear a uniform to school—maroon skirt, hemmed at knee length, and a white, pink, or yellow button-down blouse, which comes in short and long sleeves.

But every girl in the 80s owned at least one chunky cable-knit Forenza sweater. I have asked repeatedly for one, but we can never find them at TJ Maxx, so it doesn't look promising. Then one day, I am nagging again. She is likely sick of it and finally agrees to buy me one, so I would shut up. "Your father is going to be so mad at me," she mutters in the checkout line to one ecstatic owner of a new hot pink, V-neck, Forenza sweater from The Limited.

"We don't *really* have a father," Mom says. He does not go to the games and recitals. He doesn't want to buy us birthday and Christmas gifts. He will not take us on vacation—too expensive. He never wants to go anywhere, except church. We are extremely unlucky children. Thankfully, she never says it out loud—what she really thought—that he doesn't love us.

The fact is her truth is my truth. And no one, even Dad, will change my mind.

University Village apartments offer off-campus housing for students and non-students. Residents could walk to the adjacent shopping center with a Kroger grocery in the center. Dad's apartment was on the second floor. The area was generally quiet. If you drove past the apartment community, you would find yourself in a residential area with small, older houses surrounded by mature trees. But the kids that lived in the apartment below ours threw booming parties on weekends and weekdays.

Many nights, Dad pounded the floor with a hammer to subdue them. They would lower the volume of the music for about five minutes and raise it again, raising his blood pressure. Calling the police didn't help. When they arrived to inform them of the complaint and warn them to lower the noise, they feigned compliance until the officer disappeared. Dad remained powerless and returned to his pillow highly vexed.

Dad is a praying man. On his knees every night, he has made a life of it. He loves everything to do with the church. He truly loves God and seeks refuge in His house. For spiritual practice, he pours over the church fathers' writings in his spare time and reads the Bible daily. But most of all, he works and rests in the divine liturgy and the many colorful sacramental services in the church. Every window and layer of his soul, every fold of that consciousness, is filled by the church. He doesn't have any other hobbies. Rarely is he seen reading anything other than the Bible and religious books. His spiritual, artistic, and emotional experiences culminate in the church, which also colors the lens through which he defines his cultural values.

His favorite day of the year is Good Friday. My brother, Mark, was born on that day in 1978. After the birth, Dad rushed to church for the tail end of the long Paschal service. I think Mom never got over this. She always believed he loved the church more than his family.

He never consumes alcohol—ever. He refuses to take on the role of judge over anyone but himself. Personally, he believes that Christians should not drink at all, and nearly all in his family believed the same. Mom likes communion wine and can handle half a glass before announcing herself "drunk." Her word for drink-drowsiness. I think it is perfectly adorable.

Dad molds his existence to the shape of church life and spiritual practice. He moves to its seasonal rhythm and tastes the sweetness of God's word as served up by the fathers and mothers. The saints, martyrs, and early theologians are his teachers. In many things, he will become mine.

Annually, the church holds many community fasts for various remembrances or spiritual themes. He carefully observes each one and makes it a family practice. All foods and drinks that come from an animal are removed during fasting periods. In our house, the vegan rule is strictly followed during a church fast, so if sodium caseinate is listed on the ingredients label, it's out. Mom, who hates legalism, finds this to be ridiculous. "We are not Pharisees," she rags aloud. But this never alters her husband's resolve.

Dad is highly disciplined and harbors a staunch work ethic. While Sunday is predictably his favorite day of the week, he does not tire of his identically formatted weekdays. They obey the clock and operate like one. Wake up at 6:00 a.m., brief standing prayer in the kitchen, and off to work by 6:45 a.m. He does not leave the building for a break. He lunches in the cafeteria with a friend from church who also works there—home by 4:00 p.m.

A quick hello to all, mail check, and upstairs for a thirty-minute nap. Then downstairs in his robe seated at the kitchen table with his Bible to be read silently for twenty to thirty minutes while Mom cooks. World news at 6:30 p.m., followed by dinner. Sometime after that, always before 10:00 p.m., he ascends to his room for prayer on his knees and bed.

This seems a dull existence to me, but I will believe that adhering like glue to a consistent routine was as beneficial for Mom as it was for Dad, if not more. His deeply religious convictions are rooted in his childhood in Egypt. The youngest of five, he learned the ropes of ministry following around his older brothers while they preached in the villages about Christ. These ropes certainly tugged on his heart, soul, and mind, for he truly loved to serve the Lord all his days.

He tells of an early experience that jump-started his journey. At sixteen, he and his two brothers, Latif and Mourad, were in a village on an appointment. A small sermon was to be delivered for the families who had gathered to hear. Edward was not told that he would have a specific task for this mission. He was just there to help and learn. As the time was approaching to begin, Latif took him aside quickly and informed him that he would preach the message.

"What am I going to say? I have never done it!"

His brother instructed, "Ask God. He will tell you what to say."

So onward, he walked to the center of the clearing. He faced the people, but his eyes veered upward, and his mind flashed a prayer for words. Then he began to speak the parable of the prodigal son. He said the words flowed like a river, smooth and easy. His memory failed on the remaining details of that day, but he remarked that the Holy Spirit gave him the words. That is the only explanation, he said.

By sixteen, I will fiercely hate my life and secretly wish she would tell me to leave so I could say she kicked me out. I desperately don't want to make things as bad between Mom and me as they are between Mom and Dad. I still hope things will get better. And if she is the one to demand it, I can't be blamed for it later. For if she does tell me to leave, surely, she will apologize someday.

Mom doesn't apologize for throwing family members out of the house or for leaving her fourteen-year-old daughter stranded at a gas station—or for anything else she might do now or anytime in the future.

CHAPTER 6

I Read People

Dealing with Delusions
1988

Her symptoms are worse. She is more agitated than I have ever seen. Talk of psychopaths and evil is endless. She can't stop. There's no pause in the jabber, and I can't get a word in.

"Mom, these are just normal kids. They have never hurt me like that. They are mean, but not dangerous. You've never met them." There were nice kids in high school, but the mean ones linger longer in the memory.

"How can you say that?" she interrupts. "How can you not believe me?" Her voice is incredulous and tinged with a combination of hurt and anger in hot pursuit of changing my mind. These days, five minutes in, the rant is tense and shrill. If I allow this conversation to continue, not that I have much choice, she will escalate to loud yelling, angry insults, and accusations, dumping multiple layers of guilt on my head.

30

My heavy head is spinning, slowly numbing me. The rant is the same every day.

"I am your mother!"

"This is exactly what they want!"

"They want to turn you against me!"

"Are you going to let that happen?"

"Do you see how you're crying now?"

"That's exactly what they want!"

" They are playing with our emotions, woulaad el kelb. Sons of dogs."

"That's what they do."

"Have you ever seen them?" For sure, I'm going to stump her this time.

"Who? The committee? Of course not! They are watching us from their office. They bugged us. They can see everywhere in this house, and everywhere we go."

"How? It has been years. We would have found the bug by now ..."

"I can't tell you that now."

"Why not?" I am certain my brain will explode. How can anybody believe this crap? How does she come up with this stuff? In the last year, Dad has nearly turned into a broken record, reminding me that she is sick. It's not *her* talking. It's the illness. Her psychiatrist, an OSU doctor who diagnosed her, gave him those words.

"I don't know! Ask them!"

I laugh.

Mom narrows her eyes. "You think this is funny?" she scorns.

"No, but how am I supposed to —"

"They are very, very smart—much smarter than you and me. They know how to do things we can't imagine. They are very high up at OSU."

"How do you know they are at OSU? Who told you that?"

"They did."

"What?"

"That's right. *They* told me." Her wide eyes are like saucers. She is on high alert, ready to pounce as if they are about to walk through the front door. I'm intrigued. This is the first time she has reported someone speaking to her.

"When?" I ask curiously.

"I don't remember exactly."

"Was it recent?"

"Yes."

"Where were you when they told you this?"

"On the phone."

"What exactly did they say?"

"I can't remember. But they said OSU and committee," she said as if being interviewed for a story in the Columbus Dispatch. "I don't want to talk about it anymore," she said quickly.

"Okay, Mom," I mutter, mind racing.

Hallucinations? Is she getting worse? How far will this go? I must talk to Dad. Does he know? Mark and Dalya are too young; they can't hear of this now. I can't deal with this now. I want it all to go away.

"Anyway, are you going to stop talking to those girls?" She is happy to return to the original topic of our discussion. "Because you know, they are evil. Everything is planned. There are no coincidences. There is a master plan behind all of this, and we are in the middle of it. I am the subject of their study. The scapegoat."

"Why us? Why you? You're just a normal human being." I say. I receive narrow eyes again.

"With psychic powers. Is that normal?" she smirks.

I roll my eyes.

"You don't believe me? I can *see* evil. You don't believe that after everything I've told you?" The gavel is about to strike. I'm about to go to jail.

"You don't believe anything I say, why should I believe you?" I yell. "Besides, what do you care if I believe you? I can believe anything I want!" I lash out. She has an answer for everything. It's all worked out perfectly in her head. I can't convince her of anything. So stubborn. Silently, I curse mental illness. What is this hideous disastrous monster? Cancer would be better than this.

Ignoring me, she continues, "I read people. I can see psychopaths, no matter how charming they are. I can detect them. I am rare, so they want to study me for their evil experimentation. And they want to stop me from recognizing them. That is why they are dangerous. They will do anything to stop me, even kill me because I know them. They've already threatened to kill Mark!"

Rising from the table, I head toward my room. I've had enough for today, but she has not.

"Mom, stop following me," I say flatly.

"Wait." She quickens her step, resurging. "I have to tell you something else, and then maybe you will believe me. Do you remember when we were at church, and Uncle Selim was talking to your Dad? When I looked at him, he looked at me, and that's when I knew. Because he revealed himself to me by the way he looked at me. I know for sure he is evil. And now your father is talking to him, which I've told him many times not to do. He is going to brainwash him, ibn el kelb!"

"Mom, he's not … we were such close friends," I attempt feebly. I have run out of things to say.

Uncle Selim, Tante Renee, and their two daughters had moved to Columbus a year ago, and we all had become instant friends. The older daughter Mona and I had quickly become close, and Mona adored Mom. Her sister Sylvia and Dalya were forming a warm friendship, too.

One afternoon, I was chatting with the sisters on the house phone in the kitchen. Mom was there, tidying up and singing a cheery tune. Smitten by the sound of a high chirpy voice audible in the background, they demanded elatedly, "Oh put her on! We want to talk to her!" Mona, Sylvia, Dalya, and I and our mothers loved to sing. Long ago, Mom had such bright energy in her voice when she sang. It tingled your ears and sprinkled droplets of glee all over you.

"That was before he showed me who he is, and your friend." She said the word friend with a sneer. "He was saying, 'I have him, he is under my control, and I will have your daughter too.' And now Mona is going to play with your emotions, too. That's what they do." Her voice is rising.

"You loved Mona and the whole family at first! Don't you remember the first time they came over? It was one of the best days ..." That first visit with the Girguises was a sweetness we would later have to learn to savor without her for the rest of our lives. It was a day of food, laughter, singing, and bonding. I could see a joy on Dad's face that was unfamiliar to me. We had found bosom friends.

But the second time Mom saw Uncle Selim, it seemed like something switched in her brain. He entered her delusions, and suddenly, he was a psychopathic demon who must be severed from our family and avoided at all costs. Our families' sweet friendship terminated as quickly as it began. As for Mona, I was never to speak to her or see her again.

You are not going to do this again, I thought. My racing brain tried to ignore the familiar, growing pit in my stomach. *Why do you hate all my best friends? I hate you! I want you out of my life forever.* I made a secret vow. Everything else was secret —all her sick, crazy secrets imposed on me. The secrets were all around her. I will have my own. No friend of mine from now on will ever meet this woman. Ever.

Making that wordless proclamation does not mean I don't keep trying to convince her that Mona is not a bad person. Mona and Sylvia are sisters. Why is only one of them evil? You liked her before, in fact, adored her. Nothing changed between the time you met and the second interaction. She's a good person. She goes to church. She doesn't swear. She's always looking out for me. She's not charming. She can actually annoy me. I'm old enough to make my own decisions. I'm certainly old enough to choose my own friends for God's sake. You don't have to see her.

For many months, I argue every point I can muster. But she has a logical answer every time. Everything makes perfect sense to her. There are no holes in her theories. She can't comprehend how no one believes her warnings. She is nowhere near ready to accept not being believed.

Mona and I continue to hang out through college, and our dads remain friends. All encounters are hidden from Mom. If she asks, we lie about seeing any members of the Girguis family. It creates too much chaos in the house. If discovered, Mom escalates to a level of anger and screaming verbal violence that heaves a pain and crushing guilt not easily shaken. Some of that guilt will not be loosed for a long time.

"How could you do this to me!" Her voice is a hollow scream. "How could you not believe me? How could you talk to her? You are letting her win! She is brainwashing you against me! Don't you see, ya ahbeeta—stupid girl. Even if you don't understand, you should listen to me to support and honor your mother! But instead, you choose evil? Evil over good? Evil over your mother?"

"Mom, stop screaming!" Her eyes flash toward me. I can't remember for certain, but likely the words out of my mouth were not calm or quiet. "I am not choosing evil! No one is evil! I'm not trying to choose you over anyone!" I shout, then try to take a deep breath.

"You are hurting me." There is pain in her voice.

"No!" I feel the dam of emotion begin to burst. "You're hurting me!"

I can scream as loud as her. All efforts to be calm and level-headed fly out of the kitchen window with the 70s-print flowery curtains. I don't care if she doesn't understand or can't see reality. I'm sick of tiptoeing around invisible Mona in the house. I'm sick of the secrecy and the lies. I'm a good church-going girl. I lie to my mother about Mona and every other "psychopath" I have the audacity to call a friend and speak to despite her demands.

What kind of daughter am I? I'm probably going to hell. And now, I don't care. Mona was my closest friend from youth group during the dark high school days.

She pauses a few seconds, as a thought occurs to her. "You used to believe me. What happened? It was that ugly girl. She brainwashed you!"

"Stop! She is not brainwashing me. Can't you give me a little more credit than that? I'm not stupid. You even tell me all the time how smart I am. I don't think anything different about you ..."

"If she wasn't brainwashing you, you would believe me!" She means this. This is plain truth to her.

"I believe *me*. I make up my mind. No one tells me what to think. I believe you about everything else, just not psychopaths."

"You don't know what you're saying. She is evil and smarter than you and all the people around them. They know what they are doing. They are sly and deceitful and fool everyone. That's why they are after me because I know them. I'm the only one that can see them. And you should believe me when I tell you that."

A new thought suddenly occurs to me. "Why is it always me that has to believe you? Why don't you ever believe me? Why don't you ever believe anything I say about my friends?

Why are you always right, and I'm always wrong? I'm so sick of this!"

"There's only one truth," she says incredulously. "You need to accept it."

Don't I know it. And that truth is that no matter what I say, how much I plead, how smart my comebacks are, I will never convince Mom. I will never break her out of her world, nor will I change her mind about our friends. This is my heart's grating roar. More than a boyfriend, a best friend, or the latest pop-star album, I want to smash the glass bubble in which she exists. Besides, I cannot feed into her delusions. I cannot encourage them. That would make it worse.

Dad always says we should neither agree with her in the abnormal discussions nor affirm her false thoughts. He insists on this. It's as right and fair as telling me at eight-years-old that Santa Claus does not exist.

Years later, Mona will appear at my wedding and position herself discreetly in the back of the church. Though invited, she will skip the reception to avoid chaos. Our beloved Selim and Renee, who were like my second parents, will not attend at all. Their absence will be like a funeral to Dad and me.

CHAPTER 7

Somebody Trusts Me

Abby from the Continent
1989

I meet Abby in the summer of junior year at the Continent, a European-inspired retail and restaurant quarter. The Gathering is a weekly event for residents from around Columbus. They flock there for an exciting Thursday night hangout. Teenagers from all over congregate outside by the fountain. The kids stand around and chat or catch a movie at the theatre. Abby Bailey is from Worthington Christian High School, and we hit it off right away. She talks to me first. No way in a million years would my shy self be the first one to say hi. She asks me about a boy whom she knew attended my school. And that's how it starts.

She wants to be friends, and I don't believe her. She is gorgeous and bubbly. I was always told I had a pretty smile.

The rest of me is friendly, but painfully awkward, keeping quiet and watching people. She talks to the people. She talks to everyone. I love her clothes, though I could never pull off her style. She sparkles from the inside and out, and she is a little flirty, another thing I could never be. Her pale green eyes peer right into mine when she speaks to me. When she asks me questions, she seems genuinely interested to know about me. I wonder why. She is a glass of champagne. I am Lipton tea with a pinch of sugar.

I imagine her and me becoming best friends and quickly freeze the thought. Another thought creeps in. What if she's acting? What if she's just using me to get to Mom? What if she has no interest in being my friend, and I'm just part of a study by The Committee? That would explain the attention she is giving me.

The girls who were friends from my high school have recently dropped out of my life. For the first two years of high school, I had been included in the gatherings and sleepovers. We talked on the phone daily, like best friends do. I didn't see it coming on the first day of school. Melanie was acting strange and quiet at the bus stop that sunny morning. Not her usual chatty self. She hadn't said hi, or even looked at me. When I asked her what was wrong, she said nothing.

"That's not true, I insist. "Tell me."

"Nothing," she retorts. "Stop asking," she says without turning her head to look at me as we climbed onto the bus.

Every day of junior year that we had ridden the bus, Melanie and I sat next to each other. Not today. As I followed her to our usual seat, she quips, "Don't sit here."

"Why not?" I ask, confused.

"You can't."

"Why not? I press. What is happening? The sun turns black all around me.

"I just can't talk to you anymore!" She is louder now. Harsh. Mad. She won't look me in the eye. I don't dare her to.

"Why not?" I'm loud.

"I can't say. We just can't, so stop!" She sits down and stares at the back of the dark green seat in front of her. I drop myself on the seat four rows behind her and fix my eyes on the window. I stare through the glass at the trees along Henderson Road. We drive past Whetstone High. What's it like to go there? Public school. I wouldn't have to wear this dumb maroon skirt.

She never speaks to me again. The other girls in our group also never talk to me again. If they are forced to look at me in the halls or at the lunch table, it's to sneer and snarl, like wild cats. Thrown away like trash, I am struck with bewilderment. Morning suns sting me. High school morphs into a hot desert with no rain or air.

The thick glass window and the trees along Henderson Road become my new bus friends.

I have not always known that Mom's beliefs about people were distorted and that her thoughts were all in her head. Consistently over the years prior, my thoughts were one with hers. I loved her so much. Before sixteen, everything she said was true.

Everything had made sense. Mom is a psychic, and that is why no one comes to our house. They are either jealous or dangerous. Her special powers of reading people and recognizing evil are extremely rare. There are only a few in the world, if any. My mother happens to be one of the infinitesimal number of psychics. Believe it or not, you can count them on your hand. The Committee of *special doctors* at OSU are highly interested in her extraordinary powers, so they need to study her brain. Therefore, they have us under surveillance.

"Now, Habibty, this is very important," Mom once said gently, eyes widening. The coming secret was larger than life, more grotesque than an adulterous affair, more exciting than winning the lottery, more hypnotizing than a swinging pendulum. "It's not just the house that is bugged. Our bodies are."

I stared at her. No. Impossible. And gross. It's got to be illegal. No way! My stomach hurt as the words wheezed in a slow hiss.

"There is no way that can happen." I felt like I was being punished, but what was my crime—being her daughter?

"They have their ways," she said. "They absolutely can do it when they want something bad enough. And they do. They want me for their evil purposes. They are fascinated with me and my brain. And as a result, they are interested in you and your sister and brother."

Watching my reaction, she said, "I know, habibty. It's awful, isn't it? There's nothing we can do to stop them either. They are very powerful."

"Are you going to let them use you? Study your brain?"

"I don't have a choice! They're already doing it!" They are watching us right now, but you have to act normally."

I stood up and looked around. As a middle-schooler, I had slipped easily into a state of fierce self-consciousness. I thought about the condition of my hair and glanced at my clothes. I thought about my showers.

"You have to act like everything is normal. Don't show them that we know anything or that you care even if they know that we know." Her voice diminished to almost a whisper.

"They can see me in the bathroom? When I'm showering?" I envisioned a group of old men in white lab coats surveying my naked body while standing in the shower. I imagined them leaning forward in high black leather office chairs to get a closer look. They are taking notes with cross ballpoint pens on yellow notepads. They are impassive and very serious.

"How long are they going to do this?" I don't remember which feeling was strongest— nausea, fear, anger, or despair.

"I don't know. We just have to wait and see. But remember, be normal. Just act normal as if everything is fine. They're not going to do anything to you. They are studying us because they found out about me. And of course, don't tell anyone. If you tell people, it will make things worse because they won't believe you and will alienate you, and that's exactly what they want."

I could not have known as a thirteen-year-old that it was her *insistence* on the Committee, surveillance, and lurking evil being a reality in our lives that would continue to haunt and alienate my family for a long time.

For some reason, I don't remember asking Dad if all of this was true. If I did, he did not negate these ideas at the time. I was completely loyal to Mom. She was right about everything. It was because of her that I donned shoes I liked from The Shoe Works and my favorite clothes, like my Forenza sweater. She always told me I was pretty. I believed her. I didn't have a reason not to.

I felt sorry for her. After all, life was hard for a psychic who was forced to be the key player in a stealth operation to detect evil—all while almost single-handedly raising three kids with no family around and no friends.

I'm scared of what will happen when Mom meets my friends, so I put it off for as long as possible. Although I still wonder why she would want to hang around with me, Abby and I talk on the phone endlessly. But I only make phone conversations from my bedroom with the door locked. I surreptitiously hang out at her house and at the theatre Wednesday nights along with 200 other high schoolers. She lives in a giant colonial in Westerville, and her parents are nice to me. At her house, I feel refreshingly normal, and I try desperately to act normal, unsure of exactly what that looks like. It doesn't feel like anyone is watching me there. Even if they're watching me everywhere, I don't think about it as much when I'm not home.

I didn't know or believe it at the time, but Abby accepted me for who I was and proved a true friend. At the time, it was more important that she treated me like I was normal. Urgent blessings come unexpectedly. Whether we know it or not, they might be lifesaving.

I think my new friend will be different in Mom's eyes. She is completely different from Mona or Uncle Boulos. No way will she think Abby is an evil and dangerous people-user. I make the horrific discovery that I am wrong when I allow her to come inside the house for the first time. Psychosis strikes again.

"Do not see her or spend any time with her again," Mom orders the day after Abby's visit.

"What? She didn't even talk to you. We were in my room the whole time!"

"She's evil. She's a vicious psychopath. She is never allowed to enter this house again."

"No," I blurt out as my heart internally crumbles. I need some kind of surgery or glue.

"No, what? Again, you're not going to listen? You'd pick evil over your own mother!"

I catch my breath ready to respond, but her attack is too fast.

"How dare you? How dare you ignore everything I've told you as if everything is okay! As if it's not true, or do you think I'm lying? You're still listening to them!" She screams.

"It's not true." I blurt out. Suddenly I know I shouldn't have said this. I also internally kick myself for allowing her to meet Abby. What was I thinking? I should know better by now!

"Get out of here," Mom shrieks. "You're not my daughter."

"Gladly." I storm to my room and slam the door as hard as I can, but the force does not break the door off the hinges to my great disappointment. I cannot believe she is doing this. How can she steal another good friend away from me only to throw her away?

I can't understand how she does not see my pain and what she is doing to me. I am much more shocked to realize that close relatives can't see it either. In the spring of that year, Abby, who has just obtained her driver's license, stops by to take me for a ride in her new car. She waits for me. Mom's face freezes with alarm and fear. My uncle, who is visiting from Colorado, looks away from me, and my aunt glares at me. Following an entire evening of awkward silence, they instruct me firmly to never hang out with her again. For the remainder of their visit and beyond, no more words are uttered about my friend.

But they might as well bellow from the roof that I am the worst daughter on the planet. They might as well report the incident to the local police. And they might as well throw me in jail because that is what I deserve for befriending a psychopath and allowing her to encroach on our property with her evil car. No words are spoken to me about Mom or mental illness. Not one private discussion nor word of comfort occurs in reference to what is going on in our house.

And still, I cannot understand how Mom does not see even one of Abby's many sparkling qualities.

I never tell Abby about Mom's crazy beliefs.

Decades later, I would realize the irony of the reason my friend delighted me. Her bubbly personality, energy, sass, and class were not new to me at all. Unbeknownst to me, the psychosis had snatched these traits away and had hidden them deep inside my mother.

I hear footsteps in the hall outside my room. She tries to open the door, and finding it locked, demands entry. I open.

"No, that's not what I meant," she quips bitterly. "I mean, get out of here. Go live with your father."

CHAPTER 8

When Push Came To Shove

Moving In With Dad
1989

The truth is I couldn't stand living at home anymore. Wrecked by the madness inside her head, she watched and attempted control of my every move. She listened in on phone calls and restricted my phone time every day. She figured out how to make the house phone inoperable after 9:00 p.m. Teen torture. Because my closest friends were not allowed to come to the house and I didn't get invited to parties, talking on the phone was a crucial outlet, my social sustenance.

She was always stressed but not slack, uptight, but not incompetent. She frugally and efficiently fulfilled all her household duties. I mowed the lawn when I got old enough; then, Mark took over. Mom did the rest: cleaning, laundry, shopping, cooking, and yard work. She drove us to practices, games, and recitals. She arose each morning. After all, she was not depressed, just paranoid. She packed our lunches, and dinner was on the table every night. On her watch, we did not have to fend for our physical needs, only the emotional.

Later, she would say that she had been a single mother right up till we moved out. Resentfully, my thoughts would scream in return that she doesn't have to work for a living as most single moms do.

I remember Mom and I fighting. We made each other angry constantly. But that is not why I was fine with moving out. I needed to get away from the constant ear-splitting ranting about psychopaths and the OSU Committee. Discussions in the common reality, real subjects, and events that were actually occurring had diminished to almost never. I needed to create distance from her to end the screaming between us. Her thrashing voice inside my head would continue for a long time.

I was also getting away from her eyes. They scared me when she was in psychosis. They were filled with terror and bitterness and wrecked with despair. I mistook psychosis for a clean seething hatred. Did I read her correctly? I translated her general disposition to a depressing perpetual absence of hope and happiness that I believed would never return.

The windows of the off-campus apartment featured no curtains and the white walls with no hangings. I can't even remember a cross or picture icon that adorned our childhood home ubiquitously. There was a couch and a dining table. The news blared from the radio in the bathroom every morning. No pictures were taken of this place where Dad lived for five years.

I moved into the place mid-summer before my senior year of high school. Anything would be better than living with her in that house, which was jail, not that I had ever been in a real jail. But the feeling of entrapment had begun to suffocate me. Fear crept slowly. Despair took over. By the time I moved in, I was fully convinced that Mom was ill. I had to figure it out myself. *No one had spoken directly to me about Mom's mental condition. No family friend, relative, schoolteacher, or priest uttered words about schizophrenia or its symptoms—ever.*

Is she *really* mentally ill? Why Mom? Why us? Who gets this? Why are we so weird? Are we cursed? I must have said one or two of these aloud to Dad. We were sitting at his kitchen table. Gently, he said, "I didn't tell you before because you would not have believed me."

I knew he was right. Mom was my everything. She was my laughter, my tears, my hopes, my excitement. She was my yes, no, and maybe. I wanted what she wanted and hated what she hated. She believed in me, though her distorted reality made her forget that sometimes, so how could I not believe her? Her curiosities and observations were mine. She was interesting to me and interested *in* me.

She watched me. I could not have known at the time that her attentiveness was my food. As an older teen and college student, I hated it. Then I missed it—the way she looked on and spoke her opinion about every little thing—for example, that I should always neatly fold my underwear and socks and put them away in the dresser. That impatiens are the most prolific outdoor shade flowers. Comet Cleanser powder cleans best, and abortion is okay in the case of rape.

After many more turns around the sun, I would encounter a woman who would unintentionally show me just how much I prized Mom's attention and viewpoints. She will appear in a later chapter.

47

But the attentive watching over me like a mama bear turned into a close hovering like a helicopter, which then became like a prison camp, closed off from the closest people to me—my father and a few close friends from church and school. No conversation went unmonitored. Phone calls were screened. If Abby called and I engaged, a stinging array of verbal explosions ensued. Mona knew better than to call at all. This was before the time of cell phones. If the telephone rang and I was in my bedroom, Mom listened from the other receiver. If I was in the kitchen, her pricked ears tuned in.

More times than I care to remember, Mom discovered that I was still communicating with Mona and Abby. Daily, I lived in fear of those detections. The resulting accusations and threats produced anxiety and frustration that left me scared all the time. Every word was produced warily. I was done walking on eggshells.

"You're working with them against me. You would turn against your mother?"

"I'm not working with anyone. There's no one anywhere against you," I plead for the thousandth time.

"Liar! I'm taking the phone out of your room."

God, help me.

There is nothing I can say or do to change her mind about anything. She is so blind that she can't even see me anymore. Since when would I ever, in a million years, have the gumption or gall to join forces with a bunch of scary psychiatrists against my mother anyway? Does she even know me? I guess not.

Moving out was the first and last thing I wanted to do. Dad was quiet, pleasant, and peace-loving. During the fasts, he ate foole maddamas (cooked fava beans). I ate Subway sandwiches and Moo Goo Gai Pan from the corner Chinese takeout. I lived on TCBY and eventually got a job there, serving yogurt. My supervisor was kind.

I resumed attending the Coptic church with Dad. the first Sunday of my return after four years of absence, the incense caused a coughing fit, and I had to run out of the sanctuary for a few minutes. Dad followed briskly and asked if I was okay. I did not articulate how wonderful it felt to be back or how I had missed the scent of incense and our hymns and how the familiarity of our church soothed every nook of my soul. I continued to attend liturgy weekly. It was a good home for me.

Dad never missed a church service. He bounded for its sanctuary as a child runs home from school, whether the day good or bad. Church was a safe haven from his home life. He rarely complained about his wife, though I always thought he had every right. For some years, it was a difficult existence for everyone, including him. Many times, it was sheer madness. He took refuge in the church.

In the life of the church, a believer can experience incessant joy. In the weekly divine liturgy, a simple faith leads you through the life of Christ in the remembrance of sin, plea and acceptance of mercy, petition for others, the hearing of His Word, and Christ Himself in holy communion. The entire body of members is united through this faith and sharing in His body and blood. The presence of the Holy Spirit is as real as the bread and wine we savor—a regular miracle. Once, he told a new convert that the liturgy in its entirety is delicious.

He loved the church and its every aspect. A treasure box filled with gems, he had picked up, studied, pondered, and delighted in each one. The hymns, Midnight Praises, Coptic language, sacraments, Agpeya (prayer book), major and minor fasts, and feasts, metania (prostrations), writings of the early fathers, stories and prayers of the saints and martyrs were not options, but jewels to be worn daily by a royal heir to the King. He wore them dutifully and happily.

Dad's heart throbbed to the rhythm of liturgical life. Strong and steady, it was a pulse that never faded. His heart was much easier to understand than Mom's mind. The church was the primary way we connected, and it was easy because I dove right into church service and activity at a time when everything else in my life was a bleak mess.

He always served the church. He packed from life in Egypt all his knowledge, wisdom, and experience and brought it with him to America. He applied it to church ministry at St. Mary's. His largest suitcase was stuffed with humility. Though at home, he was soft-spoken, his occasional Sunday sermons boomed. When I was little, he preached in Arabic, and I wished I could understand them. By the time I was older and understood more of the language, he had stopped delivering sermons at church.

His favorite subject was the Gospel and anything to do with God. His only pastimes outside of church-related events were prayer, reading, and watching the news. He ate simply and relatively healthy. Sometimes he drank coffee and tea. Each night he ascended to his room with a glass full of ice in his hand. Each morning he ate cereal with milk, rice milk during fasting periods. A wide assortment of cereals covered the vintage tea cart in the dining room because there was no room in the pantry. My favorite was Cinnamon Toast Crunch. We never seemed to run out of Kellog's Corn Flakes and Frosted Mini-Wheats. For Christmas, when asked, he requested honey on the comb, a thing I never knew how to locate. But a pack of M&Ms never failed to please.

Dad was trained as a pharmacist in Egypt and then sent to Russia, which was part of the USSR at the time, to attain a doctorate in microbiology. He was commissioned to return and work for the Egyptian government upon completion, but, following his brother's advice, he diverted to Germany, then Canada, and finally settled in the United States.

"There is nothing here," he urged Dad on the phone. "Get out while you can. What are you worried about? Our parents? Do not worry. They will be fine," said he. Consequently, President Gamal Abdel Nasser placed Edward Raphael on a blacklist, which was dissolved years later by the next leader, Anwar Sadat. During those years, returning to Egypt even for a visit was out of the question.

The story of moving across the Atlantic was not necessarily funny. But this did not dawn on me till I grew up. When Dad told the story of his immigration, it was all he could do to get through it. Sometimes I wondered if he would ever reach the end with all the interruptions of stitched-up laughter. Nearly every fragment of the tale caused him to burst out in uncontrolled fits till we couldn't help but join. We reflexively laughed more at his laughter than the story itself. Every time he recounted the events, he got so worked up that his round face puffed up and colored bright red and stayed that way till the blacks of his eyes could barely be seen. The giggling lot of us just kept giggling till he could go on. And that's how it went until the end when he landed work at Abbott Labs in Ottawa or when he detected the only Coptic church in Canada at the time.

He said that every step in the journey was a miracle from God. One or two officials on one or two occasions granted passage without all the proper documents. There was a skipped interview and a letter from Bishop Samuel. I wish I had taken notes while he recounted the events. I ache to hear him tell it one more time with the patter of his pealing laughter.

Dad did not regret the decision to flee his homeland. The world was a mere stopping point. He was just passing through en route to his final destination, heaven—life with God and His saints and angels, free of distractions, worry, and pain. However, he intensely missed his family in the old country. Once, I pulled an old photo album out of the cabinet and asked him to identify some of his family members whom I had never met. He explained several of the small, yellowing black and white portraits, including those of my grandparents, then abruptly told me to put it away.

"Don't show this to me anymore," he scolded.

"He misses them," Mom explained when later I asked the reason for his brusqueness.

The year I lived with Dad at the apartment would become a blur to me. I would be thankful for the blur—the quiet, the escape from the constant accusations, and loud buzz of a scary world with scary people. I made new friends at church and began to appreciate Dad, toying with the idea that he was trustworthy and loved his children.

But life was still secret. Mom was still a secret. Not once during that year did I entertain the notion that I was normal nor ever would be.

PART 2

Secrets

CHAPTER 9

Fixing Her Mind

The Hospital
1989

Major mental illness does constitute an enormous loss. The person as you knew her or him before may seldom be around again. You must allow yourself to grieve this loss.[1]
—Rebecca, Woolis

The sharp, petrifying halts of life etch deep and vivid in the memory. When Mom shows up unannounced at the apartment, I am out with Mona. I don't remember where we were or what we were doing. But I do remember returning home that night with the moonless sky.

The residents of the lower-level party apartment are standing outside and stare at me as we walk up. They peer at me curiously, their faces outlined with half-smiles. I might as well be naked. They want to know the reason for the commotion that is usually caused by the presence of the police, who must have arrived just before us. They are already upstairs. When we catch up, the three officers are standing close to Mom. They grab and handcuff her, one man on each arm. They take her away somewhere. I run into the bedroom and stare at the mirror. I stand there, still. I'm unsure of how long.

A distressed Mona rushes after me. "Cecile, are you okay?" Her voice is urgent. Mine is not. "I'm fine," I say resolutely. And you thought you could make noise, noise; I silently scream at the *partiers* downstairs who had watched the entire episode. Were we disturbing you? I am tempted to run downstairs and taunt but don't.

Mom is taken to the state mental hospital on Broad Street for treatment, and Dalya moves into the apartment with us. Dad tells me later that she had started throwing objects at him and yanked the telephone out of the wall in the apartment living room. Unwilling to leave even after he warned her that he would call the police, she had screamed the entire duration of her visit. Why did she come in the first place? She had never graced the apartment with her presence before. Maybe now she will finally get the treatment she badly needs.

But I am not holding my breath.

In the United States, the law is on the patient's side when it comes to the terms under which treatment is received. They must consent. For involuntary (forced) treatment, the patient must show that they are a danger to self or others.[2] Furthermore, ten years later, before I began my research on Mom's treatment history, I discovered that they destroyed the records of her stay as part of their records retention policy.

The consent rule was a thorn in our side that pricked sharper every time Mom became agitated, made threats, or could not stop ranting. The more her condition worsened, the tighter she closed the walls around her children. Her beliefs were her reality. To her, the psychopathic predators in her life were as real as the nose on our faces. They were as real as the criminals broadcast on the evening news that she watched every day. Because of this "reality," she was in a constant state of preoccupation, alarm, and mental exhaustion.

Without medication, her ability to have a two-way conversation disappeared. We knew antipsychotic drug therapy was the only way she would be able to regain stability in her interactions with us, even if her delusional beliefs didn't change. When I say *we* knew, I mean Dad.

From him, I learned and believed medicine would calm her. But somehow, I wasn't sure that *maintaining* stability would be as simple as a trip to the hospital or a prescription. It would be better than nothing. She needed *something*. But even with that something, whatever the chosen treatment, something else inside me knew the struggle with schizophrenia would continue far beyond the hospital stay.

Mark had moved in with Dad and me months earlier of his own accord. Even at the young age of eleven, he has had enough. He sticks around when I hang out at the community pool, and he plays basketball with other kids in the neighborhood. I am protective of him and he of me. Dad doesn't cook much, so we eat frozen Totino's pizza every day. With the money I make from working at TCBY, I buy Subways two or three times a week, maybe every day—six-inch roast beef on wheat with lettuce, tomato, mayo, and extra banana peppers.

We sleep on mattresses. Dad sleeps on the floor. He doesn't make us do chores around the apartment. I blast the radio while he's at work. Once, Dad heard my sobs reverberating from the bedroom and ordered me to stop. I don't remember the reason for this. Either the tragedy of the situation made him emotionally withdrawn and more stressed, or I blocked it out. We don't talk much about the parents, but we look out for each other. Once, I yelled at a kid while he bullied Mark. He and another cohort had attempted to beat him up twice on the basketball court.

Three decades later, Mark would remind me of the reason for the surprise appearance. She had come for him. This is why she took twelve-year-old Dalya and walked 3.8 miles on four-lane high-traffic roads to the apartment on Harley Drive—to take her son back.

The look and feel of Columbus State Hospital (now called Twin Valley Behavioral Healthcare Hospital) does not surprise me. Nevertheless, the sight of stark white walls and workers dressed in white almost spins me right around and out the door. Some of the patients walk the halls aimlessly. Some sit motionless in chairs in the lounge. They look like statues. More than one screams incoherent sounds or nonsensical phrases. The staff members wear white coats. There is a stench in the communal area. Mom is given not a room but a stall in this lock-down facility. Apparently, inpatients don't get rooms with doors and windows like they do in real hospitals. Her tiny space comprises nothing but a cot and a dividing curtain.

"This place is awful, Ceci. I have to get out of here!" I don't know what to say.

"Sorry, Mom," I say. I am full of sorrow.

"I don't belong here," she says. Her voice is passionate and desperate.

As vehemently as I hate this place, I don't want her to leave just yet. I am counting on them to make her better. But by the fourth visit, my expectations have diminished.

Perhaps I am not the only one with low expectations. Dad mentions later that a few of Mom's siblings are angry with him for dispatching her to Twin Valley. Why are they angry? Dad tells me they called to announce they are coming to visit her. He tries to warn them that she would not see them and that their flights would be for nothing. There are two visits from Canada and Florida. Mom agreed to see them once. I can tell they hate it here. They hate that their sister is here. They don't talk to me about Mom or what's going on.

Another time during her stay, a bishop from the Coptic Church also attempts to visit her, also unsuccessfully. Was this kind clergyman praying for her? Would he have doused her with holy oil had she received him? Would it have helped? Has my faith become frozen along with my feelings?

I hope my instincts are wrong. I hope this hospital will fix Mom; that she will get the medicine she desperately needs and enjoy a paranoid-free life forever with no delusions ever again. Robotically, I pray for a miracle. Why wouldn't God listen? My request is a good one: to heal Mom. Make her normal. Free Dad and all of us from this monstrous disease.

Make *us* normal. Make *me* normal. These are my conscious hopes. My subconscious cry I would realize later was one that I would also not be granted anytime soon.

Return Mom to me.

CHAPTER 10

Changing Her Mind

Reason Doesn't Work
The 1990s

Mom loved her children. When we were young, she didn't often say so in those words. It was more of an emotional proclamation, something about how she sacrificed her life for us. We heard over and over how she gave up so much to take care of us. I hated it. The repeated statement made little sense, considering the seemingly opposing fact that, unlike Dad, she had always desired children. Why were we such a tax on her life?

"Your father didn't want children," she scorned.

"Why not, and how do you know? I can't believe that," I said soothingly, willing myself not to believe it. But I was too scared to ask him.

"He told me."

"Yeah, but he probably just didn't want kids right away, like he wanted to wait for a little while?" There is a small pleading in my tone.

"No," she said sternly. "He didn't want kids ever. He didn't want to have to pay for them and all the work it takes. He just wanted a wife to take care of him and do everything for him."

Whatever, I think. I refused to believe this, and later I did seek confirmation from Dad. When he heard what she said, he laughed softly. "No, that is not true. Of course, I wanted children. I just didn't want to have them right away. I wanted to wait a few years."

The better answer. This is what I wanted to believe, so I did. I deeply craved normal parents and normal life. When would we become normal?

Contradictions between my parents' statements occurred all the time. Arguably, this was common among married couples. Less common was the inability of an adult daughter to see her mother as she was in her core. Maybe I stopped hoping that she would ever manifest her long-lost inner beauty so that those who had known her before could see it again, and others, like her children, could see it for the first time.

In Mom's case, one of the wretched symptoms of delusional thinking was a gross lack of self-awareness. Mine wasn't so great either. So, I could not have known then that, in truth, I badly wanted more than anything to see Mom the way God made her and intended for her to shine. I unknowingly yearned to see the dazzling gems of her mind and heart that comprised her person. But I didn't know that. There was no time or space in our existence for such a luxury.

We were just trying to avoid discussions about psychopaths and make her believe us. Allowing for the possibility or hope that we could intimately know Lily in a normal way, know a mind on the same page as ours that could mentally adhere to the common reality, and contribute meaningfully to the community, was pure indulgence and engaging in a cruel hoax.

Dad knew very well that it would have been tremendously valuable for her to work. Fiercely independent, she would have relished having a personal contribution to the household income and the world outside of our house, the extra money would have been nice, and the sense of purpose in teaching would have been deeply filling for her. She had a brief stint as a substitute French teacher at Ecole Francais, a nearby French immersion elementary school.

The job was perfect for her as I think back. She taught young children patiently and spoke French fluently. She had to quit after a few months because of constant back pain. She couldn't be on her feet all day, but to see her working outside the home was a thrill for me. Young as I was, I remember brimming with pride over her. Whether for the meaningful work teaching a language I was smitten with or because she had a paying job, she certainly seemed important to me in a new way.

I was sad when she quit. She liked the job. I liked that she liked it and that she was working and had something to do besides cook, clean, and watch soap operas. I imagined that she and Dad would now stop fighting about money, and for sure, she would forget about psychopaths and stop talking about our family members and friends being hateful and evil.

She never worked outside the home again.

Like many people in their twenties, I thought I had it all figured out. The meaning of life, being a good Christian, my future, and my mother, who was not a mystery, just a sick person. With a mental disease, she had zero credibility, questionable judgment, low reliability.

She had let me down throughout the previous years with words. When a house gutter leaks, the water trickles down slowly, eroding the pretty garden bed underneath. Her words gnaw at me like the eroding water.

"We're not going anywhere."
"We're not doing anything."
"No, you can't go."
"We'll go to the mall, to the park, to Kings Island."
"We're not going."
"You will."
"You won't."
"You can't."
"Why are you thinking of such silly things?"
"Don't lie, ya kelba."
"Stop making this house filthy."
"You don't know how to clean."
"No, I won't make headscarves for church."
"No, we can't stop at Niagara Falls on our way home."
"At least your cousins wear makeup."
"Why don't you straighten your hair and do it nicely like them?"
"Your aunt spends all her money on herself, but I spend it on you kids."

It takes the whole duration of years-long treading hills and valleys till you realize. Till the dawning of the sun of maturity and awareness sheds light on a past spotted with negativity. They were only spots. There was much good. But the words. Words have a way of settling deep, cluttering your mind, and strapping your decisions and aspirations like a straitjacket. In that jacket, there is no movement. Without movement, there is no creation. Without creation, well, I don't remember daring to dream.

In James 3: 5-10, we are reminded, "See how great a forest a little fire kindles! And the tongue is a fire, a world of iniquity … No man can tame the tongue … With it, we bless our God and Father, and with it, we curse men, who have been made in the similitude of God. Out of the same mouth proceed blessing and cursing. My brethren, these things ought not to be so."

"You should be a doctor."
"You're good at math; you could be an engineer instead of a journalist."
"What are public relations?"
"No, I won't buy you any more piano music."
"Stop playing the piano and come and eat."
"No, you can't bring your friends over, especially that evil one."
"And don't mention that name in this house again!"
"No, I don't need any help in the kitchen."
"Your father never wanted children."
"Only I did."
"At least Mohsen spends money and buys his wife jewelry."
"He treats her and is affectionate with her."
"Mine doesn't do any of those things."
"He doesn't do anything."
"What are you talking to your Dad about?"
"What are you and Dalya talking about?"
"Where are you going?"
"Out with Mona?"
"She's not your friend."
"Neither is your cousin."
"I can't believe you went to their house."
"I don't care if she's my sister."
"Her husband is a psychopath, and so is his son!"
"Don't you understand?"

"Yes, Rasha is too. Isn't she Nagwa's daughter?"

"It doesn't matter that she's your cousin."

"You don't have to see it; you must believe me and do what I say."

"Don't listen to evil!"

Dad repeatedly told me that the derogatory statements she made toward us were not Mom speaking. She says those things because of her illness.

In my eyes, she comprised one solitary facet: being mentally ill. I might have tried to imagine her without illness, but what was the point? The memory of what she was like without the constant, carefully rationalized discourse that pressed her sinister views had faded away. I might have attempted to distinguish real Mom from sick Mom, replaying her words and actions in my mind and force-fitting them into one of the two categories. I was never certain of my choice.

Some days her mere existence plagued me, and I couldn't see beyond her warped mental state. There were days when I tried so hard to make her believe me. She just needs to hear it in a certain way, I thought, attempting to grasp air in my hand and hold it.

That would have been easier than holding her trust and getting her to change her mind about anything. The problem with Mom's afflicted mind was that there was no reasoning with it. Her delusions were her reality. To her, they were as real as the air she breathes and the sky above her head. To her, we might as well have been trying to convince her that the sky doesn't exist!

Yet I still hoped, still asked, still strove to help her see things differently. I lived at home through college. By this time, Mom had been hospitalized against her will for three months and stabilized on Haldol. She never accepted the fact that her perceptions were not real and that she needed medicine to settle her thoughts and calm her. Since the first psychiatric appointment to this day, she has rejected anything is wrong with her; Her thinking and perceptions about people and life are the reality of her life.

Dad tried. He explained persistently why it was so and why it wasn't. He used simple words to explain the common reality that everyone else could see but that she couldn't, the one that she *should* believe to be actually against the delusions in her head. He tried to reason with her, appealing to her own inclination to think things through carefully. Earnestly, he used examples that, to him, were compelling enough to change her mind. But no matter what he said, her mind would not be changed.

"He looks at everyone that way. He always has that look on his face," he said about Uncle Boulos. "It's not just to you. He gave me the same look!"

"It was only for me. And if it was for you, it was because of me," she returned contemptuously as he shook his head. "He is dangerous. You need to call the police," she persisted.

"No."

"Pick up the phone and call!"

In *The Lion, Witch, and the Wardrobe,* by C.S. Lewis, the White Witch turns her enemies into stone. They are at first alive and breathing with color and feeling. Then, at her word, they harden, motionless, gray, cold, and staunch. A person standing before the rocky figure might dance, kick, scream, cry, plead, and reason to cause some alteration in its disposition or reaction, but to no avail. Change is beyond the capability of the once animate creature.

The mind he entreated, of which he tried to purge the delusions, was as immovable as those stoned creatures. For us, it was like talking to a brick wall.

The brick-wall idiom has been used to describe stubborn behavior or to make the point that the person refuses to change their mind. The problem with using the expression to describe interactions with Mom is that she could not change her mind.

Asking her to change her mind or her perception about our loved ones being evil and dangerous was like asking her to believe that flowers are people, or that the sky is made of orange juice, that bees don't sting, or that wars do not occur on this planet. As far as she is concerned, we might as well have asked her to believe those things. To her, that is exactly what we did.

Her delusions are her reality. The common reality is elusive. Parts of it are unreachable, inaccessible. Clarity skirts between breakfast and a phone chat with her sister; it skips through the shower and an episode of *The Young and the Restless*. Glimpses of correct thinking form like raindrops on roses and in seconds splash the wet ground. Then they are gone. They slip between my smile, Dalya's smirk, and Mark's playful mischief.

I banked on those refreshing blinks of time. She knows. Down deep, she must, I purr, convincing myself as I've been trying to convince her. She can discover the truth. I can change her mind.

Reality is reality, and I knew the difference between fact and fiction, actuality, and delusion. And somehow, someway, with my healthy, intelligent, college-educated brain, I would fix hers. Let me assure you that I never "fixed her brain," and I never changed her mind, not for a season, nor for a day, not for a second.

CHAPTER 11

Time To Take Your Medicine

Help Comes
The 1990s

Uncle Selim, Mona's father, was one of Dad's closest friends. For Egyptians, any friends of parents were called Uncle and Tante, an address of affection and respect simultaneously. But he was truly just like an uncle—kind, open-hearted, and open-minded, especially for an Egyptian in the generation preceding mine. Conversing with him was like breathing fresh air. He was a good friend.

He entered her delusions soon after he and his family moved to Columbus a couple of years ago. To Mom, he was nothing more than a deceiver and evil psychopathic manipulator, a dangerous man that secretly brainwashed everyone at church against her.

She repeatedly warns us about his treacherous smile and how he uses it cunningly to turn people on with a charm so powerful that they believe everything he says. I should be very careful around him. I must be smart. Smart as him, Uncle Boulos, and all the others like them, except we are on the good side.

So, Uncle Selim and his family never come over anymore. No one in our family is allowed to speak to him or Mona, who is evil by heredity. If we want to talk to any of the Girguises, it must be a stealth meeting, kept light-years from Mom's awareness. When she catches Dad and his friend talking on the phone or at church, all hell breaks loose. Her voice was hollow and pathetic. A disgusted, irritated tone penetrates the house.

"How dare you stay his friend with everything he is doing to us? You are humiliating yourself and me! Is that how you support your wife? What kind of husband does that?" she scathes repeatedly. When he attempts a rational explanation or tries to convince her that Selim is a normal man with faults like everyone else and not dangerous in any way, her voice rises to a shrill, filling the air with heightened tension.

> "If you were a good husband, you would stop talking to him." She jabs.
> "We have to talk about things to do with Sunday School," he replies.
> "Really?" she taunts suspiciously. "Do you think I'm stupid? Like I don't know?"
> "You need medicine, Laila. Think about taking some to help calm down," he implores.
> "Why? Only sick people need medicine. Do you think I'm sick?" she accuses.

69

"You get very agitated. It will just help calm you down. That's all. Many people take medicine to calm down. It's okay to do that."

"I see! Now, he's brainwashing you into thinking I'm mentally ill. And you believe him?" Her voice is rising, incredulous.

"No one is brainwashing me." He says; his voice is low and quiet.

"Get out of my face. You're not a husband. If you love evil so much, why don't you marry it!" she screams.

Uncle Selim and Dad talk secretly on the phone. They avoid speaking in church unless she is not there. Even then, there is an ongoing fear that an observer will mention it in passing. If she finds out I've been talking to Mona, I am no less guilty, and the verbal attack on me is choking.

"How could you?" The chastisement is mixed with contempt, devastation, and finality. "How could you?" She is shaking her head. "You would do that to me? I told you that he is evil and that he is hurting me, and you kiss the devil right in front of me? Would you betray me like that? Would you humiliate me? In front of the whole church? How ugly! How could you? What kind of a daughter are you?"

Angry desperation explodes inside me. I want to keep her. I want her to love me so badly. She can't love me if she thinks I'm betraying her. I am hurting her. She thrashes me with her tongue, but my actions thrash her heart. I commit more heinous crimes. I dream of gentle hands caressing my forehead.

"I barely spoke two words to her!" I lie. "She started talking to me; I wasn't just going to ignore her and turn around and walk away!"

"That's exactly what you should do! You should never ever talk to her or her evil father."

"That's very unrealistic," I say, trying to reason with her.

"Don't you want to support your mother? You are more loyal to evil than to your own mother."

"No, I'm not. I just don't agree. That's all; she's only annoying, but to say that she's evil ..."

"See? You believe her over me! That's how powerful evil is! You aren't listening! Stop listening to evil and listen to me for once!"

"I've listened to you a thousand times. I just don't agree with you. I have my own opinion. Why can't I have my own opinion and you have yours?"

"Shut your mouth. Stop it."

She has had enough of me and I of her. She sends me out of the room, and I, dejected, am glad it's over. I internally plan to change my tune in the next encounter and tell her she's right about everything. But Dad advises against this, insisting that confirming her false beliefs will not help her.

During one of the secret phone conversations, while Mom was staying at the hospital, Uncle Selim informed Dad that he has learned of a colorless, odorless, tasteless form of an anti-psychotic drug they could get. It was called Haldol. A mutual friend and psychiatrist agree to write the prescription, though he was not her doctor. Dare we do it? Dare we be happy?

That summer, Mom was an inpatient at Twin Valley for ninety days, the maximum length of stay permitted by the hospital. During that time, Dad and his three children moved back into the house on Winterset Drive, and I prepared to begin college in the fall. I was glad we were home but uneasy about Mom's reaction to Dad's return. It's not as if he asked for her permission. Once, he mildly complained of the expenses. "For five years, I paid the mortgage and rent at the same time," he said, shaking his head. It was his only complaint related to the apartment.

A year later, Dad fervently asks me to help him manage her Haldol intake. As an eighteen-year old, it is now my mission to protect Mom from discovering the secret operation of dropping it into her food. Dad says Mom's family and my siblings can never find out. It would be the end of everything if Mom ever caught us. Along with Dad and Uncle Selim, I also bear the responsibility of protecting the psychiatrist, who is not her doctor. Ultimately, I must protect Dad, who sneaks this wonderful drug into her food every day and swears me to absolute silence. It's as if we are walking on tissue paper with a bottomless pit underneath.

Treading every possible path to get her to seek help, we had exhausted every option. Dad and at least a couple of Mom's siblings had suggested, pressured, and pleaded with her to take some medicine. The doctors had very little to no influence as they, especially the psychiatrists, had entered her delusions and were therefore dangerous and never to be trusted.

We tried to keep the reins of her own care in her charge and uphold her right to consent to all aspects of treatment. After all, this was the ideal situation for a consumer. But to no avail. Nothing worked. She accepted no kind of treatment related to her mental health. Because, of course, she didn't need it. She was not sick. Every time it was mentioned, a volcanic uproar occurred, and the trust between her and those that loved her the most crumbled more and more with the days and years. The unavoidable reality was that without a solid treatment plan that included medicine, she would only degenerate.

No one can know. Shhh. Not a word.

CHAPTER 12

Secrets: Our Second Language

Shame, Isolation, Division, and Walls
c. 2000

The face is the mirror of the mind, and
eyes without speaking confess the secrets of the heart.
—St. Jerome

Dad used to say that it was because of her sheltered life that Laila got sick. Nuns practically raised Mom in private schools in Egypt. Out of the eight Makar children, she was the only offspring to enjoy that privilege. The others attended public schools. The family even relocated once to a town that offered a private school so Mom could enroll. Many times, Dad said that the sheltered environment of private school and being confined at home might be the reason she developed a mental illness.

There is a story of a woman who has special powers that are beautiful and dangerous. Out of fear, her parents require her to hide her magical powers because of an incident that almost kills her younger sister. The magical sister then spends her life wrestling with the secret and fighting to suppress her growing powers. This chilling and exquisite aspect of herself entraps her in the castle, and she lives secluded. Day after day, she tragically pushes her younger sibling away, cutting off all communication and crystallizing a solitary life complete with fear and angst that uncontrollably extends beyond the castle as her powers set off an eternal winter.

The younger sister also knows what it's like to grow up essentially without her sister—alone and hidden with no one to talk to—while living together in the same house.

This isolated magical sister is the woman I unwittingly idolized. Her mind was a dreary haze of isolation and fear, so her life was. My entire conscious memory of her is riddled with the hopeless dread of lurking danger.

Reason and reality are not part of the equation. For Mom, and consequently her children, our family was in a constant state of being ridiculed or hated by almost everyone. The lack of reason and a firm grip on reality spilled over onto us kids, so we, to varying extents, became like these sisters.

The story of Mom's first trip to the hospital in 1989 was one of the sharp freezing points in the Raphael kingdom. No way on earth would I tell anyone that Mom went to a hospital for crazy people. Worse yet, she was forced, thrust forth by big

74

scary men with badges. To my sixteen-year-old self, it was a frightening place, where fear drenches the suffocating air—a place void of feeling and warmth, a place of death.

Lily was there for three months, during which a mere three minutes dragged endlessly. I couldn't stand that she was there, let alone the reality that she needed to be there because she was not in her right mind. The secrets were just as suffocating. No one was talking about it, and no one could know. Her admission to the state psychiatric hospital was an admission of hers and our contemptible state. I thought that we must be a disgrace to our families and our community. By the time I was married, I had stopped allowing friends to meet her. I barely spoke of her. I was ashamed of her.

At twenty-four-years-old, when I got engaged to an OSU graduate student from Bath, New York, and an active member of our church youth group, I panicked a little. George Bibawy had only lived in Columbus nine months, during which I concluded he was the one for me. There was something about his warm smile and quiet demeanor. He knew all the long spiritual hymns chanted in church, and, as a learned deacon, he drew me with his voice—low, steady, and strong. What would he think when he learned of the schizophrenia? Would he break it off? On a youth trip to Toronto, I consulted a former confession father who knew our family and about Mom's illness. Father (Abouna) Severus had married my parents, baptized Dalya and me, and fortunately knew George and his family well. Abouna had become one of the forbidden when Mom began claiming that he was an evil psychopath. When I asked him what to do, he assured me that George was not the kind of person who would be scared away. He advised me to give him a brief description of Mom's condition without including too many traumatic details. That is what I did.

"Your dad's faith, and yours is amazing. It makes me love you even more," George answered as I let out a giant sigh of relief.

But I had more concerns. Would he enter her delusions and be cut off? Would she try to stop us from getting married? Being the most gentle and pleasant man on earth, how could she view him as evil? Mom had already met George many times and liked him. By the time he moved to Columbus, she had been on the Haldol for seven years. Her demeanor was calm, and rants about psychopaths were rare, so our youth group could hang out at the house without incident or embarrassment. But would the wedding be stressful enough to trigger psychosis?

Because we would be living in Rochester, we held the wedding there. She was happy for us. Several times, she said, "He's a good man, Ceci. You're marrying a good man." It was one of the few points on which Mom and Dad wholeheartedly agreed. If Mom had been wrong about every person in her life, she wasn't wrong about George. His love for God and attachment to the church reminded me of Dad. But for Mom, it was his love for me that satisfied her. "Make sure you become good friends with his parents," said she. "They are good people."

One exceptional risk we took was inviting Abouna. But to my amazement, she was merely appalled. "You're going to invite a psychopath to your wedding?" said with annoyance only to Dad and me when George wasn't around. To the further knowledge that Uncle Boulos also planned to come, she only said, "I don't care." This was when I began to classify psychotropic drugs as miracles from heaven.

Among the two bishops and five priests who officiated the wedding, Abouna Severus would be the one to deliver the sermon at our request. Mom never said a word to me about it.

The miracle medicine maneuver compounded the secrets. At Dad's fervent request, I protected our stealth operation using the eyedropper of Haldol in her food for fifteen years. He had gradually coaxed her into the daily habit of drinking a small glass of orange juice. This alone was a considerable feat and the catalyst to the enjoyment of more than a decade of peace. Right before dinner, he quickly pulled the white bottle from his coat pocket in the closet, which was in the hallway off the kitchen, added the liquid to the glass, and added the juice. Sometimes he asked me to do it or distract her while he did it.

His worst nightmare was that she would find out, for if she did, the sliver of trust between them would be gone forever. She would guard her food like a military protects its fort and again descend the spiraling mountain of hallucinations, delusional outbursts, screaming relentless demands and insults, and escalated terror. Hell, all over again. I was worried about Dad being on his own now that I had moved away.

A decade and a half later, when George and I moved back to Columbus with our two little ones, I felt a nagging sense of duty to tell my younger sister and brother, who by then were in their mid-twenties. At first, Dad rejected the idea. Too risky. I left it alone for a while, but it wouldn't leave me.

I was sick of the secrets. Keeping this crucial information from my siblings is criminal. Shouldn't they know now? Aren't they old enough? Couldn't we use their help? Shouldn't they be aware of the real reason for the constant tremors, dry mouth, and weight gain? Isn't it time for them to understand why Mom has been relatively calm all these years and why our family has been able to stay intact?

I was sure they would be happy that Dad was able to obtain the miracle medicine and keep Mom stabilized. I reasoned they would appreciate that because of this stabilization, only possible with the medication, we were able to avoid more hospital stays and bouts of crisis. They'd be thankful for God's provision in our lives. To all my questions, he shook his head, but finally and reluctantly agreed.

Our father was not in the room when I told Mark, who promptly exploded. Incredulous that neither Dad nor I told him all those years, and that we had essentially tricked Mom into taking meds, he stayed angry for more than a year. At first, Dalya denied that it happened at all. When she finally accepted it, she threatened to tell Mom. Dad and I had committed a grave injustice, she said. We were not on Mom's side and never were. She must know the truth, she said.

"We have to tell her. I'm going to tell her," my conscientious sister announced. She would do right by our mother. She would treat her right and stop the deception perpetrated by Dad and me.

I begged Dalya. "Please," I said, with every emotion in me. "There will be a war. Everything will be lost. Lily will be lost. She will never trust Dad again. She will hate *me*—this time forever."

But this loyal daughter saw herself as Mom's only true friend. If the rest of the family continued to act as her enemy, Dalya would be the one to stand up for her. Payback for all the time, Mom called me an angel, I suppose. She didn't budge.

The world dimmed and lost color. The birds disappeared. Humidity swarmed. Silence deafened me. But the calm that is supposed to precede the storm eluded me. I already felt the sky dropping.

A few days later, in one conversation with Dad, Dalya agreed for his sake to wait till after his death to tell her. When he passed a few short years later, she wasted no time. She told Mom without warning Mark and me first. This act cut a deep rift between us. Secrets do that. They cut and divide.

"That's impossible," Mom said, first in tears, then stoutly. "Your dad would never have been able to hide something like that from me. He didn't know how to be sly. I have never taken that kind of medicine. They want you to believe that I'm sick and that your father did this. Even your father. They tricked him."

Dad had slipped quietly into history, and her unstable mind settled the secret forever. It never happened.

When a girl grows up in a kingdom of isolation, she becomes a queen of fear, awkwardness, insecurity, intimidation, and shame. My ability to trust people froze to towering ice glaciers. I ceased talking about my life and family, especially Mom. I would not be my authentic self nor share my feelings honestly. The risk was too high. Vulnerability was a bad word. My desires and dreams were silenced. Going "all in," especially in friendships with women, was out of the question.

Without trying, I had gotten comfortable inside my cold walls. You can't engage when you're hiding. What kind of mother would I be to baby Juliana? Wonderstruck by this little miracle that had sprung from George and me. What was God doing? Was He sure He should have entrusted me to *mother* a soul? And three more would come! What did I know about being a mother? Admittedly, I would ruin them.

The secrets had taken their toll. As the years would pass, I would not only hide myself but my mother, too. From anyone outside the family and very close friends from church, she would remain my deepest secret.

CHAPTER 13

The Peacemaker

Legacies of a Father
2004

Faith is not just to be mentally convinced but is an action
inside the heart, to lead one through his whole life.
—*H.H. Pope Shenouda III*

A few nights before Father's Day in 2004, Dad awoke in the middle of the night, unable to breathe. Within minutes, the paramedics appeared in his bedroom. Then he was in an ambulance—pneumonia. Four days later, chatting in the hospital room with my parents, Dad suddenly started gasping for air again. A muffled speaker voice emitted from somewhere above me, then a dozen people dressed in scrubs materialized.

A woman with short brown hair dressed in a long skirt and sweater is walking toward us. Why is she wearing a sweater in June? She is gently ushering us out of the room into a nearby waiting area. We had sung his favorite parts of the Coptic Midnight Praises in his room the first night while unconscious. I don't understand. The doctor had reported that he was improving. The next day, he told me that he hadn't heard us, probably because of the drug therapy.

Five minutes later, another woman, whom I gathered to be the doctor working on Dad, walked quickly into the empty lounge and sat down next to Mom. "I'm so sorry," she said with feeling. "We weren't able to do anything else to revive him. We tried everything we could. I'm very sorry. No, he's not coming back ..."

My vocal cords were muted, but my brain begged God to help and screamed at the woman just doing her job. *What are you doing here? Go back and revive him. You're the doctor, for the love of God. You can fix him if you hurry. Can't you see my mother crying? Go! You're running out of time!*

Time has a way of doing that—running. Some people say time is a gift. To me, time was a thief, cruelly marching onward in the wake of Dad's death, not having the decency to pause out of respect. There were days I awoke scared the memories of him would march right on with it. All at once, I intensely needed to remember everything. It was urgent. But over the years, I've realized that I don't have to remember every single thing he said and did. To keep his memory alive, I share important things again and again.

God does not get tired of raising the sun every single day for millennia. He doesn't get bored with reminding us of the essential things. (John 14:26) Thanks to Dad, I don't get tired of hearing them.

Dad relished the mysteries of God. "His wonders never cease," he'd say with love for His Lord infusing the words. But he, himself, was a bit of a mystery—perhaps because he was so quiet. However passive, however indifferent he appeared to Mom, he was a pillar-praying force holding up the fort. He was a silent warrior for soul-cleansing, a fighter, and winner for peace. He put on Christ. How could he lose? How can anyone lose if God is on their side?

Some days it seemed evil was winning—as if Mom is not so wrong. But Dad always knew better.

Truth, goodness, and beauty are found in clinging to Christ and loving His people. Dad loved his wife, who wouldn't or couldn't love him back. He was smitten with her while she was repulsed by him. He chose to love her until the end, while she seemed to reject him daily.

He suffered while no one seemed to know. Almost alone their entire marriage, he never complained. Though he had every right, he quietly bore the pain and ridicule, prayed and prayed, trusted, and loved.

I don't know if she was ever aware, but Lily needed Edward to survive this world. But she kept nothing of his. There is no picture of him in her room or purse. He is dead to her but lives on in their children. This is why we all wore white at his funeral. It is one of the precious few points of consensus the three of us had ever shared up till that day—the decision to wear white clothes in a sea of black. In our grief, we chose to celebrate his feast day—the day of his departure from this temporary place and entry into his eternal home in paradise.

Maybe in some mysterious way, Mom accepted Dad's love, just by doing her wifely duty. For nearly forty years, she washed and folded, hemmed and mended, cooked his favorites, cleaned the house, and fretted over his headaches and high blood pressure. Maybe because of her limited mental condition, the mechanical pattern of her giving, a regular, steady, cloudy rainfall of giving, was the only way she could return his love—and mine.

If I could just learn to close my eyes and drink it in, let that be her way of loving me. Like a prolonged, soft, pouring rain, filling up the riverbed and flowing out to still waters.

The mystery of love. How does it unfold? How can you get to the inside of it when it seems like love, like massive, swift hail spurts, crashes down on your head and cuts you? Love hurts and heals. It's a risk and a river flowing with peace. How do you get that peace? Faith, Dad's first legacy.

With a mustard-seed faith, taking a love-risk won't take away your peace. So, the Lord said, "If you have faith as a mustard seed, you can say to this mulberry tree, 'Be pulled up by the roots and be planted in the sea,' and it would obey you." Luke 17:6

For Dad, love was extraordinary and free. The way he loved Mom was his second legacy. It mirrors the way humans are loved by the Lord, with a passion that makes no sense but keeps us alive when we would otherwise die hopelessly. "For God so loved the world that he gave his one and only Son, that whoever believes in him shall not perish but have eternal life." John 3:16

My brain cannot fathom, but there's more to me than my mind. And there's more to Mom than hers. Thankfully, Dad was acutely aware of this. Our being can't help but receive love, whether it knows it or not. The deep part of us is designed to absorb God's nourishment like the new addition, our second baby girl, drinks from my breast.

Now what? How will I continue to be a good mother without Dad's counsel? How will I know what to do? In March, George, four-year-old Juliana, one-year-old Anastasia, and I had moved back to Columbus. My hometown sky greeted me with a picture-perfect fluffy white snowfall the day we made the drive. At my request, George had obtained permission from his supervisor at Gulfstream Aerospace in Savannah, Georgia, to work remotely. After two years in Rochester and four years in Savannah, where Juliana and Anastasia were born, I wanted to come home close to my family—especially to Dad. It was just so much easier to talk to him at the kitchen table than on the phone. But he died in June—three months later.

What is his opinion about time-outs as a way of disciplining children? How much television is okay? How do I teach them the Bible? How will I get them to love the church as he did? What would he think of homeschooling? What if I'm just too tired to cook and clean? What if George and I have a fight? What if one of the kids gets mentally ill like Mom?

The journey of motherhood would turn out to be a recurrent but straightforward lesson in trusting God above everyone. Dad's death was the bootcamp of that class.

Dad was soft, walking wisdom that wore a smile and loved the cross. He was a sort of *Mr. Miyagi* who expected nothing from people except virtue, integrity, and hard work—good, strong seeds. The stories he told were not of himself but saints and family. More legacies—the passing on of greatness before him, more magnificent than him. Despite the seemingly faint existence held in our family, the lives he touched filled the church to maximum capacity. The packed funeral service at St. Mary's testified to his profound impact on the community and beyond.

Juliana, Anastasia, and the two more who will come later will make it a habit to urge for more stories about little-girl me. Amelia will perk her ears, Gabriel will settle into his usual listening position, Anastasia will lock her wide eyes with mine, and Juliana will cock her brow, waiting. One of these days, they will get tired of the same two or three tales, like when I tried to "remake" gross rice pudding that Mom placed on the table and ended up dousing it with sugar, ketchup, barbeque sauce, and banana peppers. How they love that one.

I have dug deep and wide and have come up with some dirt and a few seeds. They seem like nothing now, but there must have been life in them once—sweet, tender, colorful fruit and flora, like the tiny faith-seeds Dad planted in us.

Edward understood people. He didn't have to know a person very long to sense their character and commitment to the important things, like God. He understood us. A few months before his death, he dropped a bombshell when he shared privately that he was concerned about Dalya's mental health. "I'm afraid she is going down the path of your mom," he warned.

"Don't even say that, Dad." was my feeble appeal.

My long-lasting denial of his hideous prediction is a little ridiculous, considering that I had read the statistics. As if I didn't know the chances of developing schizophrenia increase if a family member has it—by ten percent.[1]

Not Dalya, I decide with steely grit, as solid as a politician's promise.

PART 3

Surprises

CHAPTER 14

Discovering A New Passion

The Zumba® People
2015

You have turned for me my mourning into dancing... and clothed me with gladness, to the end that my glory may sing praise to You and not be silent.
—Psalm 30:11-12

T hey danced wild and free.
People inspire people. Sometimes it comes unexpectedly, like a lightning bolt. The love of a thing that makes you start loving yourself when, whether you knew it, you were doing anything but.

Mollie and Debbie were the instructors of my first Zumba class. They were each motherly in their ways and made direct eye contact. They gingerly checked on the students, subtly corrected improper form, and demonstrated moves after class. Danae, their sidekick, started the butt slapping, which, to my shock, didn't bother me.

Because I had no dancing experience and had always been shy, awkward, and self-conscious about my body, I placed myself for the first several months in the back of the classroom where I hoped to go unnoticed. I knew I would get the moves wrong, step in the opposite direction, and dance offbeat. I barely heard the blaring music as I concentrated intensely on mimicking the movements. After a while, when the moves became more familiar, I began to listen to the rhythmic music. Then it started to seep miles beyond the eardrums into my soul, where I simultaneously inhaled pure joy and exhaled the thrill and blaze of a thousand suns and ten thousand moons.

This kind of high-energy, mood-lifting girl time was a phenomenon to me. The life of parenting, homeschooling, teaching Sunday School, and growing our family swept me up. Gabriel and Amelia had arrived nine and six years earlier, and our four children collectively swept me away. They held me captive not only by their miraculous existence and unending questions and adorableness but because of my burning urgency to do right by them.

Before anything, I was a mom, and they needed a good one. This meant I had to keep them safe from the world and read every possible book that would teach me how to be the best mother in history because, on my watch, history would not be repeated. They would not endure the anger, neglect, and insanity that I did from my mother. They would have an affectionate, involved, and normal mom, and, for the most part, they did. I had beseeched God for mentors, and He provided. At the perfect time, I found them in the dearest and only Coptic homeschool family at church and in the moms of a new Classical Conversations community in Hilliard.

Mom had remained stable for six years after Dad passed on. But when Mark got married, she began to talk louder, shunning his new wife, Penelope, to our gaping dismay. The aggression returned. We became alarmed when she started to toss the groceries that Mark brought onto her front lawn and stopped taking her thyroid and blood pressure medicines. Finally, in 2011, when she threatened her son with a knife, he called Netcare, and she was admitted involuntarily to Ohio Hospital for Psychiatry.

She would be admitted again in 2013 to Mount Carmel West, where she was "quite irritable and uncooperative … somewhat hostile" with "poor insight and judgment." Highly suspicious and agitated, she told the staff she knew they were all involved in the conspiracy and needed to protect herself. There were witches and demons in the ward, and they were going to cast a spell on her. She said that negative supernatural forces were experimenting on her by placing a chip in her body to study her thoughts.

Unable to stabilize her, this hospital would discharge her after three months to Scioto Pointe, an inpatient skilled rehabilitation facility. There, it took an entire year for them to find a medicine that would work. Haldol had lost its effectiveness, and Invega injections seemed to work the best. Her doctors were inaccessible to us during her stay at Mount Carmel. Meanwhile, Mark and I obtained court-appointed co-guardianship of Mom's person and estate, sold the house on Winterset Drive, and found a nearby assisted living residence where she moved in May of 2014. Living alone was out of the question.

For the last ten years, my primary focus was on everyone's physical, mental, and emotional care. Where was my self-care? Missing. My family, church, and homeschool bubble popped when I started going to the gym. Two-mile runs in thirty-degree winters waxed too cold, so George suggested a membership despite my uneasiness with the intimidating environment. I vowed to plug in headphones and stick to the treadmill—until I heard the music wafting from the studio back by the lockers. Coaxed by the gym owner to give it a try, I walked into the class intending to sample no more than ten minutes of Zumba glued to the back wall. I stayed for six years and counting.

The Monday night class kept a culture of uplifting each other. Mollie and Debbie summoned class-wide support of participants struggling with their health and shared their successes. There were regular reminders to maintain a judgement-free zone—no room for a critical attitude, only for rallying and respect. Everyone was free to let their hair down and dance their hearts out.

Debbie made eye contact from the stage and poured over me all manner of genuine encouragement every class. She layered her support and acknowledgment of each participant's progress week after week until she had unwittingly crafted an exquisite, elevated, fuller version of her class members.

One day after a year or so of Zumba dancing, my favorite song on their playlist began to fill the room, and I prepared to get lost in the dance as I had dozens of times before. My earlobe felt her breath out of nowhere. "Get up there," she ordered playfully.

What? Do you want people to stop coming? I thought nervously, as I glanced at Mollie to see if she agreed. She was already nodding and tilting her blonde head toward the raised platform we affectionately referred to as the stage.

Because it was discouraged in my family, my only prior experience dancing in front of others was in middle school. The eighth-grade girls were trained to do a routine for "The Lullaby of Broadway" for the spring talent show. I was awkward and shy, but the choreographer placed me in the front, probably because my five-foot stature would have scarcely been seen otherwise.

I vaguely remember the quick thrill of a real stage. The director selected a tune that was upbeat and catchy. Mom said I did a great job. She said I looked beautiful and sexy. At thirteen-years-old, I could not apply that word to my body, no matter how good the choreography was. I remember mentally rejecting it, but I never forgot it.

I walked toward the stage with utter inability to process what I was doing. I had danced this Bollywood song a hundred times on the gym studio floor, sometimes in the front row. I never tired of it, nor do I still as I teach it. Bollywood, pop music from India, fits Zumba moves aptly, works the waistline, and is favored by the instructors, so they often include it in their playlists.

Debbie grabbed her phone to take pictures while Mollie previewed the first moves to lead the song. As I jumped up next to her, I frantically considered jumping back down to the crowded floor, but Debbie had moved into my spot and was smiling reassuringly at me. I believed, undoubtedly, the members were questioning the validity of this class and prayed they would not watch me. Mollie winked, "You got this," as we began. I stayed slightly behind her so I could see her better and focused on relaxing and dancing this routine that I adored.

I am sure I went the wrong way at least twice and lagged the beat. My brain screamed, *You're cramping her style and confusing the students*. Mollie's smile screamed back, "Keep going! Look how much fun you're having up here!" I glanced down at Debbie, whose face beamed.

The truth is that I was having a blast. The Bollywood song's duration is four minutes and forty-three seconds, every second of which I twirled, pumped my arms and squatted without noticing the ground under my feet. By the end, I forgot that the participants were watching me and only awakened to it during all the clapping and high fives. Thank goodness. After class, we took pictures while tears filled my eyes. Overwhelmed with joy, I had discovered a striking thing that night—a new version of me. "You found you," Mollie texted later as I wondered what the kids would think.

The following year in May, on a pinky swear, I registered and attended the one-day training to become a licensed Zumba instructor. The two who had inspired me from the first day dropped in by surprise at the day's end just in time for the group photo. Mollie surveyed our class of more than one hundred new instructors and chimed, "Look at all the Zumba babies!"

Ana and Ale, who had been mentored for several months by Mollie and Debbie and had been dancing with us at Kore 7, our Sunbury gym, added to the excitement of having a growing Zumba family. In another year, our little Zumba clan had grown by two more instructors, Danae and Michelle. With all their support and love, it did feel like a family. The seven of us were the Z-Sisters.

We played at the same jams so we could learn and teach songs together. We ate together and exchanged Christmas presents. We knew each other's favorite Zumba songs and favorite foods. I had unique names chosen for each of them because they were so precious to me: Sassy, Familiar, Habibi, Hangry, Fiery, Mami—their colorful strokes are brushed in me, too.

After every class, I wished I could take them home with me. Three nights per week after work, after kids, we darted to level and danced happily. We matched Zumba-brand clothes, rocked village parades together, and spread Zumba love with our class members. We not only danced at the hip, but we were also joined at the hip.

Experience breeds confidence, and confidence breeds growth. The only exception to the joy and fulfillment of being a Z-sister was when we went our separate ways. Gym membership dropped, and the classes slimmed. Ana and Ale were not receiving their paychecks. It was time to look elsewhere. We all found other gyms to teach the Zumba we loved and spread that love to more people.

Growth breeds change, and change leads to a new creation—a new outlook, new dreams, new experiences. As Rick Warren said, "There is no growth without change, no change without fear or loss and no loss without pain."[1] But pain does not have to be a one-way trip to misery.

Despite the warning signs, I was confounded when a single day after I was hired to teach a new class at Kore 7, the gym abruptly closed. Debbie, Michelle, and I had found work at a gym in Marengo while Mollie, Danae, Ale, and Ana secured teaching spots elsewhere. I loved having dancing partners and watching new members fall in love with this exhilarating form of exercise.

We missed co-teaching with our Z-sisters, but it was pure fun until a year later when the Marengo gym closed abruptly. I knew more opportunities would come, but it was lonely. I would learn later that loneliness is not a thing to fear, and it is not a constant feeling, as rain is not the endless sky. It comes and goes. When we must, we keep right on dancing in the rain.

Prayers gushed into my bed. "Lord," I appealed, "fill the hole. Change my situation. Use me for Your glory. You always do. You always make it right." Two hires in two gyms later, that is precisely what He did.

"Fly, baby, fly!" Mollie commented on my Facebook post announcing the first day of a Saturday class I would be teaching at the new gym in Sunbury, Metro Fitness.

But I couldn't shake the sadness. At 3:30 a.m., into my iPhone's notepad, I typed a draft for a blog post about friendship. My struggles were the framework of the walls I had built to protect myself in my kingdom of isolation. But I was thinking that God didn't want me to live that way and that maybe He was using Zumba to tear down my bulwark. The last thought I jotted down was that the walls come down because love came down.

Then, in the morning, He replied. It was the first line of a book of devotions I was reading at the time.

Oh, that you would rend the heavens and come down. —
Daily Light on the Daily Path, July 29[2]

And in the same entry:—

Part Your heavens, Lord, and come down; touch the mountains, so that they smoke. Send forth lightning and scatter the enemy ... Reach down Your hand from on high; deliver me and rescue me from the mighty waters ... —Psalm 144: 5,7

I wrote back, "Lord, You'd not only tear down my walls but the vast heavens to smoke, and You'd shake the mountains to save me. That's how much You love me. That's love, come down."

With my Instructor license under my belt, my dance was just beginning.

CHAPTER 15

Figment of My Childhood

Mollie's Colors
2015

Color is my day-long obsession, joy, and torment.
—Claude Monet

The first time I noticed Mollie's dancing, I knew I wanted to move like that. Wild and free with feeling. She had a way of connecting with everyone in the room. By the time a song ended, you had moves like Shakira and were convinced you looked like her. The lack of walled mirrors in the room aided tremendously to this haute self-perception.

Wouldn't you know it's a result of brain action? Mirror neurons, a discovery of the 1990s, are "a type of brain cell that responds equally when we act, and when we witness someone else perform the same action."[1] If you are taking a walk, and your child topples from his bicycle and skins her knee before

97

your eyes, you cringe fiercely as if you experienced the pain yourself. When you watch a person gag while eating, your stomach turns. The research has helped explain empathy among humans, the challenge with autism, and, ironically, schizophrenia.

"When we are dancing, and our participants are watching us, they have neurons firing in their brain that makes them think that they look and feel the same way we do."—Zumba Education Specialist Loretta Bates surmises.[2] The intense emotions of joy and passion Mollie and Debbie exuded on the floor became a part of my own experience. Zumba people do much more than dance and sweat together. They intensely *feel* together.

Mollie moved around like a butterfly while the music vibrated. In a blink, she'd appear straight in front of me with the moves, dancing as if it were just the two of us. Sometimes she smiled right into my eyes and sang me the words, regardless of whether she knew their meaning. Most of the lyrics were in Spanish.

When she connected with me in class, a mysterious ecstasy occurred. Pure bliss. Complete unabashed fulfillment that I could not explain and thought very strange. Were any of the other dancers affected this way? I would eventually understand the reason, but it would only come through a dark dance of abrupt leaps, desperate reaches, and slow, meticulous turns.

Before my first gym hire, I taught Zumba to ladies from my church in a rented space while some of their husbands played indoor soccer. It was my first class and first time learning alone. The sweet ladies and a few of their little daughters covered the windows with poster roll, and we rocked the room every Sunday for a few months. After the first class, I floated into Mollie and Debbie's Monday night class, excited to tell them about my first full-hour solo teaching experience. Mollie attacked me with one of her bear hugs before turning on the music and asked breathlessly, hands lightly squeezing my shoulders, "Was it fun? How'd it go? Do you feel good about it?"

It was the feeling in Mollie's voice, how she spoke, and the way she squarely penetrated my eyes. Was it yesterday? It persists so clearly in my mind, the intense familiarity, like a deja vu. Where had I heard that emotional vigor before? At the time, I couldn't place it. I didn't have the mental capacity to do so anyway because I had to deal first with the explosion of my feelings. I needed time. Meanwhile, I silently vowed not to meet Mollie's eyes again. Numerous times, I failed to keep that promise.

The familiarity only intensified at ZinCon. Zumba Fitness holds a convention every summer for licensed instructors to receive training, licensing, new choreography, and inspiration from specialists and jammers globally. Thousands of Zumba enthusiasts gather and have an unforgettable four-day blast. It's a bunch of grown-ups out to play on the Zumba playground. We are not thrill-seekers, just music-lovers and dancers trying to spread the love as far and wide as possible. I vividly remember Zumba Advisor David Topel's trumpeting declaration. "We are a stunning force of multicultural happiness in this world. We insist on shining a light in the darkness."

The Orlando Convention Center becomes home to nearly 7,000 participants, so our group stayed close together in the main halls during jam-packed events. One afternoon, thousands pressed into a fitness concert. We agreed to form a chain to avoid getting separated while worming our way through the dense crowd. I grabbed Debbie's hand, and Mollie held mine with light, bony fingers as our line formed. Her grip was firm enough to keep me from letting go so I wouldn't get lost in the throng's tight shuffle.

I didn't see it coming. My stomach turned. My heart plunged into a hole somewhere under the floor of the corridor during the five-minute walk. It wasn't fear or anxiety, but inexplicable bliss. The grasp of her hand melted mine till I couldn't feel it anymore. She might have been still walking on the floor, but I was floating on a cloud. I wanted to break free and bolt to my hotel room. Simultaneously, I dreaded when I'd have to let go. She would never know either. What was it about her hand?

It's positively awkward. Mollie was my Zumba mentor, not the Archangel Michael. The sticky truth from which my mind and heart could not tear away was that I didn't want her to leave my side during the entire weekend. Her mere presence was a comfort to me. I couldn't stand it because I didn't understand it.

Additionally, I assumed the same was true for her. I had never been clingy and abhorred the thought that I was just that. She endured my pettiness the way Mom would have— with swift annoyance followed by understanding and speedy return to the way things were. I remain grateful for that.

For me, the next couple of years would constitute a lengthy trial of getting out of Mollie's hair for both of our sakes. Not that she ever expressed a desire to keep a distance. I needed time to come to terms with her real purpose in my life, a mission that stretched far beyond Zumba instructor.

I loved Mom, and I hated her. Mollie unknowingly made me aware of both realities. As a result of adoring Mollie, I discovered a sincere, genuine love for my mother. It had always existed—hidden away in the deep crevices of my heart.

Mollie didn't cause my pain but caused me to *feel* all the pain. All she had to do to accomplish this was to go about being herself. Sometimes I hated her more than I loved her. What did she do? Nothing and everything, including hold my hand with one that looks and, from some distant point in once upon a time, feels like Mom's.

Mom was a figment of gray, and Mollie was a figment of my childhood. After realizing Mom's person was tainted with mental illness and a constant state of delusion, I ceased being able to see Mom's soul somewhere along this path of life. She gradually became colorless to me. Knowing Mollie splashed vibrant hues on the portrait. I could finally see Mom's colors. Dazzling shades of passion, emotion, affection, nurture, quick decision, bold opinion, wit, and calm. I had lived most of my life with black and white vision and saw color for the first time. I saw a profusion of color. Mollie was my restorative lens.

Mollie held it together. The roof could cave in, and she'd get right to doing what needs to get done. I have often wondered how much Mom could have achieved had she not gotten sick. She did all the shopping, cooking, cleaning, laundry, yard work, driving us around. She baked the fluffiest yellow cakes with chocolate sauce from scratch for our kitchenette birthday celebrations. Mom made it on regular days. She checked our clothes to make sure we looked decent and clean.

She bought beautiful furniture, mostly from yard and estate sales. My room was pink. Dalya's was white. To Mark's everlasting chagrin, his walls were covered with dark olive green and orange tulip wallpaper, which had been used to cover up their artistic crayon displays of toddlerhood.

She did what millions of mothers do every day—sacrifice. She thought little of herself and did what was needed to feed and clothe us and make us feel good when she had the mental space to do it.

Her world could have been an exciting place. She could have taught French to thousands of little ones. She might have completed hundreds of more landscapes, even sold them. She might have had girlfriends. She might have charmed the world with her playful friendliness, wit, and high-class taste. She could have fed many more stomachs with her delicious food and many more souls with her green thumb. Hundreds of houseplants garnished our home and flourished for decades. While checking her house one winter while she was an inpatient, I discovered a tangerine tree in her dark garage, bursting with bright fruit. It died soon after that in her absence.

Similarly, Mollie baked the cookies at Christmas time, cleaned for sick friends, and tended one of the prettiest gardens I had ever seen—hers. She was full of charm, wit, and perfectly playful. It was easy to see Mollie's talents and formidable ability to manage life and make things happen. Though these always impressed me, I didn't realize she was not the only one in my life who possessed a green thumb and a fierce resolve to push through life's storms.

Sometime after sunrise and a little past sunset, she could mother: boxed lunches, cleaned house, cooked chicken and moloukhia, argued angrily, strolled the mall, watched soap operas, Oprah, Three's Company, and Family Feud. Mom also held it together as much as she could.

Despite her mental fog, she persevered for us. She naturally lived in the moment, a thing I find very difficult to do. Sometimes, when she was not agitated about psychopaths, she was completely tuned in to us. But I never realized this until I met Mollie.

Noticeably, Mollie lived in the moment. When she was with you, she was all in. She absorbed every detail of her time with you. She was aware of your mood, observant of your clothes, hair, and jewelry, and listened intently to every word you said. One of her ways to communicate was with physical touch. She was always patting and caressing to give assurance, kindness, and affection. She is a nurse, after all.

I was drawn to her attentive ways and saw them as pure whimsy. Until I experienced with her these behaviors that I ingested like warm milk, I did not realize that at her core, Mom was the same. Mollie showed me a glimpse of something that perhaps I had been fed long ago, before the age of remembering.

She showed me a breathtaking glimpse of Mom without the gnarling ogre of mental illness. She revealed to me my mother's colors.

And if they could meet, which they can't, but if they could, I think they would like each other—unless Mollie entered Mom's delusions and was branded a psychopath, shunning her from her life. Then Mollie would brand Mom as crazy and me as weird, and that would be the end of our friendship. They will never meet. Ever. That is a risk I'm just not willing to take.

CHAPTER 16

Imposter

When a Person Becomes Your Drug
2016

Numerous autumns have had me claiming that there's little more amazing than the majesty of vibrant color, deep and mellow, like sun rays spilling through stained glass in a cathedral—fall's rainbow.

One of these glorious days, Mollie and I were sitting on the quaintest park bench in front of the cutest antique store across from Graeter's Ice Cream in Uptown Westerville, and somehow, our conversation topic drifted to Mom. I am not sure how it happened, and if I had been more alert, I would have craftily steered it in the opposite direction. As soon as I told her that she was not allowed to meet my mother, I vehemently wished I hadn't. That she thought we should schedule a visit and immediately said so did not change my mind.

Even when Ruby, my therapist, George, and Mark, agreed with Mollie's idea, I insisted against it. I had already splattered the dreaded words all over the table before her— schizophrenia, paranoia, anger, fear, conditional love. She might have headed for the door. "You'll be called a demon, or at least weirded out," I argued. "You'll walk out as the others did," I said. Should we be whispering?

She, of course, didn't flinch. I searched her eyes. "You'll still be you," she said. "It doesn't matter what she thinks of me. You'll still be the same." I didn't understand, but sometimes trust must override understanding.

By the morning of this planned 15-minute visit, one hundred knots coagulated in me— one for every soul I had pushed away over some 25 years, including the one sitting in my passenger seat.

I knew it too well. Same old pattern, same ancient tragedy, written on page after page of my life story, turned slowly, quietly, unnoticed. My one hundred friends were lost to me because Mom had stolen them away with her madness, or I had pushed them away with my fear. There was no way of knowing how she would receive a close friend of mine now that years have passed. Did time mellow her? No one is safe from the invisible unflinching grip of her paranoid delusions, no matter her age. Even the best medicines don't erase them. No person associated with me is immune to entering the muddled mess of her mind where reality and illusion collide. Thankfully, by mystery and miracle, and unlike Mark's family, George and the kids never entered her delusions.

My friend and I and my hundred knots rode the elevator to the second floor, knocked on the door, and I held my breath and spoke as the words ran together into one syllable. "Mom, this is my friend Mollie. Mollie, this is Lily." The three of us laughed and talked about Zumba for twenty minutes, and twenty times I told myself to let Mom see our friendship. Twenty times I silently commanded myself to let her see and stop being scared. Every minute my brain yelled, *Be yourself. Let her see you have good friends despite everything. No more hiding.* The knots came undone as we walked out. "We're still friends," she declared. "Let's go get lunch."

Mollie struck me like lightning in a late autumn storm. In a split-second, she awakened something in me. For many months I couldn't figure out what was happening to me. Sometime that year, I realized it started when I joined her Zumba class and kept going.

In a split-second, she flashed a familiar view of my mother that had been stuck, buried, hidden in the darkness of delusional confusion and fog for most of my life. She showed me how to live in the moment. When you were with her, she embraced you, enjoyed every inch of your being while she was with you. Movingly observant, she fed me.

When you become emotionally dependent on a person, you find yourself demanding their time and attention in an unreasonable, irrational way. Because of this co-dependence, it eventually becomes impossible to imagine life without them. You cannot stand it when they spend time with other people, even their family members! And the time you do share is never enough.

You think you love them, but the attachment is not caused by love. Nor is it caused by a healthy, mutual connection but by an insatiable hunger rooted in unmet needs in childhood. In his book, *How to Break an Addiction to a Person*, Howard Halpern calls it "Attachment Hunger." "The essential similarity between addicts, whether their addiction is to a substance or a person, is a sense of incompleteness, emptiness, despair, sadness, and being lost that he believes he can remedy only through his connection to something or someone outside himself. This someone becomes the center of his existence, and he is willing to do himself a great deal of damage to keep his connection intact."[1]

Mollie became a fetish, an addiction. Unbeknownst to her, she played the part of Lily — parts of Mom I hadn't seen or felt since I was little, if ever. She wasn't about to allow Mom's illness to obstruct our friendship. I was consciously grateful and unconsciously defenseless against this beautiful mom-imposter. Because back then, I didn't realize that in many, many ways, she was just like her.

Halpern writes, "It is the return of memory. It is an emotional reminiscence of a much earlier time... the feelings are as alive and as intense now, when they are triggered into your awareness by the loss or anticipated loss of a meaningful connection, as when you originally felt them."[2]

Before knowing Mollie, I had forgotten or perhaps had never been conscious that Mom had once been fun, flirty, encouraging, and loyal—all traits that embody Mollie. The difference between her and Mom, apart from Mollie's lack of severe mental illness, was that she voiced her recognition of my assets. Once Mollie told me that she loved me for who I am, not my "performance" in a fitness class. This blew my mind—the words—*I love you for who you are.* I didn't know if I could ever believe her.

Standing at the kitchen stove or in my bedroom, my mother understandably didn't believe me thousands of times because of her inability to trust. But she also didn't believe *in* me when I was young. She did not think or foresee much of what I could do. I didn't become a doctor, engineer, or lawyer, so I didn't amount to much.

I told my fetish-friend not to worry—that I did not want another mom. But I had not known that I was lying. Against every fiber and all pride, I did, and she was the perfect replacement because, in personality, she was her reflection, but better. She wasn't sick.

She was just as fun, witty, nurturing, attentive, dedicated, empathetic, bold, stubborn, strong, perfectionist, opinionated, commanding, intuitive, and engaging as my mother once was.

She was magically and tragically *familiar*. That's why I tried so hard to hold on to her. It is also the reason I had to let her go. Around Mollie, I was continually euphoric and in utter despair at the same time. If I had been a drug addict, she would have been the heroin. "When your attachment hunger is being satisfied in a relationship, you are likely to feel extremely happy, even euphoric. When it is not, you may sink into despair and depression."[3]

The moon audaciously smothers the sun's golden light in a rare astronomical phenomenon known as an eclipse. With the kids and millions of others, George and I dashed to a place we could witness one in 2017. We gazed upward with those funny, protective glasses as the moon hid the sun from view. *This is what happened to my heart.* When I was with Mollie, my state of bliss was eclipsed by fear, anxiousness, and doubt that she was real, that her love was real, that I mattered to her as intensely as she mattered to me.

It was blissful and painful to be around her. I was perpetually confused, and I sunk into depression. But the lessons I learned about myself could fill volumes.

The long struggle with a person-addiction taught me that:

- Just because time with a person feels rapturous, doesn't mean it's good for me.

- If it's an addiction, it's not really love.

- My struggle with addiction is rooted in emotional separation from my mother in childhood and other ensuing incidents.

- Attachment hunger is a thing.

- My friend, whom I once thought perfect, is not.

108

- No person on this earth can ever take Mom's place, no matter how badly I wished they could.

- I don't need my friend to make me a complete, worthy, and fulfilled person.

- No person can fill up the hungry inner gulf of love or any missing thing except Jesus.

- That it hurt deeply to leave her didn't mean I loved her, but that I was an addict in withdrawal.

- To break from addiction, ties to her had to be cut.

Leaving Mollie would punish me, but I knew it was the right thing to do. Any creeping doubts were really from my infant self and had nothing to do with my current reality. "The ending of your current relationship is, in truth, no threat to your life, but only feels that way because it arouses emotions from a more fragile time. If you survived then, you can certainly survive now."[4]

Discovering person-addiction as a known occurrence that can be explained was comforting and assured me that I was not crazy. I learned that as much as I adore her, keeping a distance was the only way to truly break free. The unhealthy attachment to her was a precious "Isaac" that God asked me to tie up and hand over. Despite my usual ambition to be obedient, this time, I thought He was asking too much.

When the walls of my heart came down after I discovered the self-confidence and that I can love in volumes, I couldn't have imagined that God would take that same heart He opened and fill it with Himself. I couldn't have known He would break my eclipsing fears and unblock the view of His light, joy, and overwhelming love—revealing a better and brighter me. But at the moment, I wasn't ready.

Tantalizingly nurturing, Mollie fed me in my dark, foggy void. But maybe I fed her. Perhaps my need helped her in the way of which I am unaware. After more than a year of unsuccessfully tearing myself away from her, she would support me again from the beginning to the end of a new battle that would shock us. Then, through a combination of moving to separate gyms and willing myself to do it scared, I would stop asking to meet for dinner and refrain from going to her fitness classes. I would finally leave her alone.

CHAPTER 17

Dancing In November

Depression
2017

*The storm readies itself to daunt me, to haunt me,
but when it comes in November, I am already greeting
its violence and rage with fierce joy and light steps. The
happy energy in me eclipses its ominous loom. The calm
of my storm's eye is the pause in the music, and my head
turns slow. My eyes close and rest on you—my elusive
love. I breathe it in and breathe it out—your tumultuous
ways. You trap me till I can no longer breathe.
You rivet me.*

*You are not even here, yet you hold me captive. I'm stuck
in the yearning of your embrace. You are not here, but I
can see you. I relish the idea of you and me, but I cannot
stand you. I crave a perfect you, but that doesn't exist.*

Hope for long days skipping with you in a meadow of
poppies tortures me.

I dance on, skirting slow and quick. My moves obey the
music, and I welcome its command. The music knows me,
so with my feet leading, my body follows.

I will dance until the torture ends.
Then, I will dance some more.

—*Written by the author*

After a few years, I might have tired of it, but Zumba
dancing didn't get old.

My Zumba quantum leap stirred my soul and changed
me more than I could have ever imagined. My heart bounds
with my feet, spinning around, stepping left, right, merengue,
slowing down to two-step cumbia and tired leg, and moving
together with the instructor and each other, but not exactly
alike; we're all different.

I turn in my little shell—like I spin on a Zumba floor to a
catchy rhythm. The music summons me, powerful, passionate
enough to stir every fiber of my soul, re-ordering the intricate
pattern of my jumbled thoughts. From deceiving beliefs that
press a girl to the ground to airy wisps of flight and freedom.
From the muddled muck of stress and confusion to pure whiffs
of clarity and balance.

Fly, baby, fly.

It was a November evening in 2014 when I sampled a
Zumba class for the first time. I didn't know that three years
later, I'd be facing the class, leading women to shimmy and

shake in front of a mirror and not wince at the sight of their bodies.

Just one voice from the place of negativity was all that was needed to whisper softer than a morning breeze, "You can't. You're not fit, pretty, skinny, or coordinated enough." I nod furiously, "You're right, absolutely—" and get my last workout by dashing out of there like a bat out of hell, never to be seen at a gym again. Ever. Thankfully, nobody said that, and I returned, again and again, solidifying my new passion. In Zumba, I burned real calories, lost actual weight, and found some real and fun friends.

Sprouting from dry, barren soil of secrecy and pretension in childhood, I wasn't used to real. I was used to fake and didn't know it. I hadn't realized that superficiality in relationships had become second nature to me. When I began to believe that the hugs, smiles, and compliments were real, something in me broke. I didn't know three Thanksgivings later, I'd be thankful for the wreckage. When the precious little around you is real or happy, but everything looks good on the outside, it gets hard to breathe. You don't realize you're surrounded by icy walls and ceiling and no windows.

Allowing myself to trust that laughter with the Zumba people was a thing we did together, and not a thing we did at my expense, caused me to see what I had missed out on—what life was like outside my glass room. Mollie danced right next to me without a flinch, Ana said I was good at the belly dance moves, and Danae said she thought I'd be a good instructor. When they all treated me as an equal and normal, my glass room shattered into a thousand jagged-edged pieces. I lost ground and danced right into the air. I could finally breathe, and I could finally cry. But then, I landed barefoot right atop the shards, and they pierced sharp.

The breathing spun into deep sighs and long, deeper bouts of sobbing. The next life chapter opened with depression. The hole I crawled into every day was dark and lonely. The thought of buying groceries, shopping for and wrapping Christmas gifts, making a sandwich, or teaching a math lesson exhausted me. I was used to juggling the budding capricious lives of four children, an aging mother who would not take her meds, and one harried homeschool in the country.

I didn't understand at first. I rushed to Zumba almost every other day, ecstatically dancing with leaping feet and heart. Class was always fun. Learning the exotic rhythms, pushing myself to squat lower and jump higher, and getting infused with inspiration from Mollie, Debbie, and the others made Zumba the happiest place in the world. But the minute I reached home, my emotions switched from utter bliss to utter despair. Mood-lifting serotonin was not all that was released. Deep sadness spilled all over my pillow after class every night. My sobs didn't make sense. What was happening to me? Why was I so sad?

I quickly got comfortable in my hole with my pen, my music, and my dark. Nothing mattered. Everything faded, even hope. In the darkness of summer, I prayed to God and wrote to Him about everything, including Mollie, trying to make sense of her.

In my daily devotional, God Calling, an old comfort, He wrote back.

Rest. Remember, I am your physician, the healer of mind and body. Look to Me for healing, for rest, for peace.[1] *—God Calling, August 16*[th]

And again, in September on precisely the right day—

I am your Savior. Not only from the weight of sin but from the weight of worry, from misery and depression, from poverty and problems, from weakness and heartache. Your Savior—like a child in her mother's arms, stay safe, and at rest.[2] *—God Calling, September 3*[rd]

114

The earth kept spinning while my selfless George caught the balls and assumed a juggling act. His life quickly turned into a crash course in multi-tasking. He was the edge of the cliff I clung to in despair because there was nothing else to do, including letting go. He held me tight.

Birds stopped singing, freeing sound space for my faint sobs that consumed every inhale. The flowers didn't sway in the sun, and I could no longer hear my children laughing. Every movie saddened me. Every sad song told my story, and every happy tune was chattering nonsense.

At various random moments, I clasped Amelia's warm, ruddy face and intensely proclaimed my love to her. "I know, Mommy," she answered with words and giant molasses eyes. My lanky boy returned my spontaneous squeezes with "I love you." His winning smile made the sweet buttery words linger just a little longer.

"How are you? Feeling better? Call anytime." Friends' mouths were moving, but I could hear no sound. I knew the words puffed out, hitting the invisible wall, and dropping to the ground. I knew what they said as they stood outside my enclosed world, lips moving, arms reaching, George smiling sure. But grief drowned out the sound, and the silence deafened me. Impatiently, I waited for this monstrous dejection to fade while wading through my days in slow motion, but tenaciously, because every single doing and dialogue is forcefully etched from a place of anguish.

So, I dragged myself to Zumba class, and still, while doing the six-step salsa to the liveliest tunes, tears appeared out of nowhere and filled my eye sockets, blurring my view of the instructors. Mollie always kept her eye on me. She didn't let me hide in the back.

On the day I took my first antidepressant, two Novembers after my first class, I received another letter from the Lord in God Calling.

Forget the past. Only remember its happy days. Wipe the slate of your memories with love, which will erase everything in which love clearly had no part. You must forget your failures and those of others. Wipe them out of your memory book. If you do not forget the sins of others, and I carry them, then you add to My sorrows.[3] —*God Calling, November 8*[th].

I loved and hated my crystalline cave in which I could see my people, and they could see me. I could not hear them. Empty, bright, pristine, sealed tight, safe, trapped, mute, and tense, I had built it for me. The antidepressant Effexor helped me cope with my symptoms—chronic fatigue, lack of concentration, deep sadness, and memory loss—so I could get my bearings and focus enough to do the exercises assigned by the therapist. In the meantime, God would slowly bust down my walls. He was clearing the way for another kind of monster that will encroach my being the following November.

But in order to forget, first, He would make me remember.

CHAPTER 18

Fixing My Mind

Facing the Past
2017

*The Lord is close to the brokenhearted and
saves those who are crushed in spirit.*
—*Psalm 34:18*

The stale wintry Ohio sky turned into a fleeting spring
with the white bleeding heart that returned in the front,
a summer garden full of tomatoes and peppers out back and
a quick orange-brown fall and Honey Crisp apples from a
favorite muddy orchard. I thought my own wispy bleeding
heart wouldn't make it back, but it did.

George and I and the children skipped around Disney,
Juliana and I saw Celtic Woman, and dyed our hair at the
salon for her sixteenth birthday. I tutored a class at Classical
Conversations in Lewis Center and dissected the world in
maps, good books, and a cow's eye with enthralled budding

teens. With a license to teach Zumba classes, I danced with strangers who became my friends.

The year aged and furrowed its brow as I saddened more and more with the days.

A double rainbow brushed away the dark summer clouds and turned the sky into a canvas barely big enough for it. It was slippery not from rain showers but from my river of tears rushing down into hours and hours into months.

The flood inside me rose higher and higher, and I, flailing, knew I was drowning. What do you do when the Nile isn't long enough to get your ache stretched across? What do you do when the dam of dark memories breaks? That year? I darkened, not just from the sun but from depression and anxiety.

My short-term memory had already been slipping while the more profound, longer one grew cleats, and I was afraid my whole life was slipping. I couldn't tell you what happened yesterday, but thirty years ago? No problem.

The old biting stories were newly vivid like that rainbow. My boy, Gabriel, asked me to tell him a story from when I was a child, and I secretly panicked for the forty-ninth time. He wanted a funny tale. He wanted to know his mama better. He tried to get closer, and I've been running away from the stories my whole life. They've been locked up in the upstairs closet of the house on Winterset Drive since I walked out.

Remembering can sadden and gladden. It can choke, and it can soothe. I used to think old painful memories were forcefully excavated from dark ocean floors. But these brooding uninvited reminders boiled up to the surface with minimal prodding from me. This year, remembering was a kick in the stomach.

Attacked continuously by grief, I pressed Ruby to explain the reason and tell me how to make it stop. She was critical to unlocking the mystery of my sadness and memory insurrections. While it was grueling to remember, it was inexplicably effortless. Events, conversations, disappointments, and losses

I had buried long ago returned to me. I remembered things I didn't know I could and never expected to again. My mind spun countlessly through a revolving door of history and the present, questions of right and wrong, episodes of pure embarrassment, hot and loud arguments, and disturbing cold wars.

It's what I did all year—remember without meaning to. It all tramped back, invading my present. Or did I go back to my past? Whichever the case, I wanted to vomit the past onto the floor of Ruby's office and walk out forever. Time machines are the stuff of fantasy.

But God is the Creator of time and sees the past, present, and future. He knew about the closet and turned me into a time traveler. Because He was coming after all of me, and He knew I needed to remember.

For his writing assignment, Gabriel composed a story about two men who travel through a portal and into another world where friendly dragons and children play together. But the Deadly Fire Blasters appear out of nowhere to fight alongside their army of evil dragons, capture the good ones and throw them and the children into the dungeon.

I'm like those two men, treading a dark portal and its outlying path to a bleak place I've been before. I must see someone I would rather not see. I'd instead be stuck in a dungeon with Grodd, who's not a dragon, but a freaky, mind-controlling gorilla.

Having left her long ago in that lifeless colonial on Winterset Drive, I'd vowed never to look at her again. I know she's pathetic, and I can't stand what I've yet to see. How will she look, how is she coping with misery?

I forget to breathe as I inch and push through. It's beginning to look more familiar. I search untamed in the dark for the closet. There it is. The old 1970s door tucked at the end of the narrow hall is smaller than I remember. I don't bother turning on the light, so I just close my eyes, push my heart-shaped key into the hole, and turn the knob.

There she is—a shivering, shriveling shadow. She's weak, stubborn, and alone. I can't see her eyes, and I'm glad. I've come to slay her when I need to love her. But I do neither. I only cry in the dark with my sixteen-year-old self. I hold her tight in my arms for as long as it takes to unleash—to remember—almost thirty years of un-cried hurt.

And while the tears fall, the stench rises out of the noiseless wreckage. She's surrounded by everything else. The wild anger, shock over lost friends and family, the ache of sadness, embarrassment, abandonment, humiliation, neglect, shattered dreams, old hopes, and old memories meant to be sweet turned bitter by the rind of disappointment. The odor of my mother's meanness and jealousy smokes. No one's been allowed in. Her heart has been surrounded by high stone walls that are beginning their fall.

The clamor of the crumbling grows as I finally turn on the light.

The stink turns into a perfume of acceptance and embrace. It was not only my mother who emotionally abandoned me. I did too. When I stuffed it all in the closet: the meat of me, the best part, was thrown in there too, like the baby with the bathwater. I hated myself.

But I'm still breathing, though in tiny ripples, so I say to my sixteen-year-old self, "I've come for you. It's over now."

"This is all I know," she trembles.

"Just you wait, it's much better now. You'll see." I finger the heart-shaped key in my hand, tracing the edges.

"I'm comfortable here," she persists, but her voice falters.

"I know. But real love, giving and taking it, is wall-shattering. You're going to really love now. You can't love it here. Besides, I need you. I've always needed you; you're the best part of me."

"I'm the weakest and most damaged part of you."

"You're going to become the strongest," I show her the key, but she doesn't see it.

"Not without a mom. I need her. I need a mother's love."

She is so young, needy, and broken. She wipes her eyes, which never meet mine. Can I love this mess of a girl? Do I have it in me after all these years? I waver. A bolt of fear strikes, threatening me.

"I want her to hold me tight and tell me she loves me," she pleads. "I want her watchful eyes to be keen, and her voice gentle and assuring. I want to take walks and hold hands and plant one of her thousands of flowerpots with her. I want to watch her paint. I want all of her. Most of all, I desire her to want all of me. I can't just let her go."

"I'm not leaving without her."

Heart sinking, I speak slow and steady. "She might have lost you, but Love has found you ... and He'll never leave you—ever."

This God we have with the lightyears-long, galaxy-wide arms reached out and picked me up from the closet and sat me down in the Zumba time machine, of all places. The dancing Zumba people are the heart-shaped key that opened that heavy closet door. For some reason, they believed in me when I didn't. They saw a person I couldn't see. They saw the girl in the closet and invested in her. They loved all of her, even the shriveled part. Now *I* see her, and I'm finally beginning to love her.

But I had one more push to do before breaking out of my dark, cramped, stifling cocoon of existence. One more return to the past to thrust one more thing into the light. Then I would be free—the good times.

Not my idea. "How am I going to find those," I whine to Ruby. I'd rather search for a needle in a haystack. Less painful, much easier.

"Write in the journal about all the happy times and positive aspects," she said. "Then you won't attach dysfunctionally to it," she said. "You won't co-depend," she says. "You'll see yourself without the identity of others you think outdo you because you'll see there was good in your life too, and that good is the reason you're here now."

What good? I wonder.

Almost more difficult than rehashing the trauma, remembering the good seemed an impossible task. But I knew it, clear as crystal. Resurrecting dead positive memories would allow me to claim them as my own. I had not done that on purpose. Only misery had been the embodiment of my experience.

Was I trying to create something from nothing? Nothing comes from nothing, as the song goes. I hadn't known that I didn't need to. In me lay a hidden foundation that was just mine—now to uncover it.

So, gathering up my year, I word-drew the neat pretty piles and the ugly messes of the last twelve months because we were made to remember. The God of love and a heart of love will never forget, and it won't always feel good. Sometimes, some years, like my 2016, buried memories will burst out of the closet and fire up the pain, refining you, rekindling your heart so it can breathe love again—healing love. Love that heals begins with self-love. I had not known loving myself was the first crucial step. Until I stopped self-loathing, I would never be able to embrace my mother.

Loving without bounds will be dangerous and miraculous. It will gain everything and lose everything. It will bind up a heart and break it. Whichever path it blazes, it will go on and on, and so will I.

Opening the closet door and embracing the trapped young girl inside opened me to new self-love and a brand new world of people everywhere. Without shame, I would tell the world about me. Without fear, I would step into the clear. There would be no more secrets, no more hiding.

It's just a start, but finally loving the deepest parts of me, I would stand outside that dark closet of shame, close the door, and forever walk away.

CHAPTER 19

Remembering and Recovery

Mixed Up Memories of the Good and the Bad
2017

It is not an external enemy we dread.
Our foe is shut up within ourselves.
An internal warfare is daily waged by us.
—St. John Cassian

One recent Christmas, I gave Mom a bracelet. Mollie had shown me these pretty things in a little accessory shop at the mall. I hadn't given her a gift in a long time, but I wanted to make this already bright season glow just a little more, so I gave it to her and smiled, saying, "It's for you. I hope you like it." And I meant it. She keeps to herself every day in her one-bedroom at the assisted living facility, and she lives with very little assistance—except for the meds. Besides frequent visits from her children, she lives alone.

It felt good to give it to her. Tiny buds of forgiveness must be forming inside, though, at the time, I wouldn't admit it. I was trying to do as Ruby had instructed. After facing the bad, the next step was to remember the good.

Mom focused on one thing at a time. If she was cooking, all focus was on the cooking—no side conversations. When she planted her impatiens or watered her pots, that is what we talked about. I guess multitasking wasn't her thing. But the house was clean, the clothes were washed, and the food was good—except for the peanut butter and jelly sandwiches in our lunch boxes. Gross. At least she never subjected us to the cultural imposition of foole madamas pitas at school. But honestly, fava beans and tahini sauce make much more sense than peanut butter and jelly mixed up together.

We did have a reasonable consumption of hamburgers, French fries, spaghetti, chicken noodle soup, turkey on Thanksgiving, apple pie, and ice cream. Mom's favorite was chocolate, but our freezer was always stocked with a box of Neapolitan so everyone could be happy.

She laughed easily, especially at Mark's jokes. She cried quickly. She cried when former President Jimmy Carter lost the second-term election because "he was an honest man." She talked of how she detested animals, then played with our little Shetland sheepdog every day. She looked right at you and smiled, holding your glance, holding you captive, convincing you that the smile was her warmest and just especially for you.

We ate dinner together—every evening after the world news. Nearly everything was acceptable for discussion. My parents did not shy away from controversial topics. Dad was always ready with the church's view. Mom played Monopoly with us, and Mark always won. I remember playing Trouble with Dad a few times and him letting me win. I watched soap operas with Mom for years, and we talked and talked about those evil people in the show. Villain Roger Thorpe in *The Guiding Light* was a psychopath, just like Boulos, Selim, Mona, and Abby.

Private conversations in the family that did not include her did not occur in our house.

"What are you all talking about?" she almost demanded on sparsely serene evenings, seating herself comfortably in her spot at the kitchen table. If Dad attempted a man-to-man conversation with my growing brother, she had a thing or two to say about whatever it was. One eye on the skillet and one ear on their dialogue, she inserted, "Why are you telling him that, Edward? That's not true," she'd snub, shaking her head. She was tender and bossy all at the same time. She was controlling, especially inside moving vehicles.

Driving with Mom made life very interesting. If she wasn't driving the car from the driver's seat, she certainly did from the passenger.

"Slow down!"

"Did you put your signal on?"

"You're too close to the car in front of us!"

"Don't look at me, look straight ahead!"

"You don't need to take the highway to go there."

"Do you know where you're going?"

"No, don't look at the map!"

"Don't eat while you're driving."

"Don't talk—that's too distracting."

Today, we are both nervous wrecks by the end of the five-minute trips to the grocery store. Cruise control, an evil invention, was never used because it took power away from her and gave it to the car. "Cars are dangerous machines," she counseled.

She spoke her mind no matter what anyone thought. She did not care. If you didn't like it, too bad. It sounds much worse when quipped in Arabic. She would follow up with a raised eyebrow and her signature look that says, "What are you going to do about it?"

She never uttered a genuine "I'm sorry," except in sarcasm or half-baked. If she liked you, you were her world. If she didn't like you, you were given the silent treatment or death stare. I drew from both sides of the stick.

In brief moments and seasons, I was tempted to rekindle the belief that she loved me for the eighty-ninth time. Fleeting wispy glimpses of feeling loved. Like the time she and I had a tickling match when I was little. Or the time she told me I'm a good mom, a thing I never allow myself to believe. And the time we cried over Dalya together. Dalya, the little sister who had broken my heart, whose heart we had broken.

Good times. Mark's very existence was one of them. He unfailingly kept us laughing with silly jokes and teasing everyone. Because he always lightened the mood, I was glad when he was around, especially when he was older, and I was in college. Ever the life of the party, he had many friends. For years, I marveled at this. How did he acquire such a keen knack for connecting with people, while Dalya and I floundered in social discomfiture? Was it just genes or personality? Or was it because Mom was very affectionate with him when he was little—more so than with Dalya and I?

I knowingly introduce the question of nature versus nurture here. A much bigger debate about schizophrenia reaches back nearly a century. What causes this condition—genetics or environment? The discourse continues, but since the 1980s, while Mom's symptoms escalated, the biological evidence for schizophrenia has been overwhelming. Additionally, scientists now say it is the combination of genetics and environment that plays a role in the development of the disease.[1]

As adults, the topic of what caused Mom to get sick would come up frequently, but not always easily with Mark. He didn't always want to discuss it. Sometimes, when I wanted to know what he thought, he quipped a short response or changed the subject altogether. There were times he angered when I tried to hash things out. With maturity, a degree in social work, and some years of working in mental health, he became more open to talking about it at a level beyond just complaining and venting. It was almost as if my hard questions placed pressure on him.

For Mark, education helped lessen the fear of stigma, minimize spreading false information, and urged his engagement in the discussion. Mark has never pursued ongoing therapy for himself. He dealt with his childhood trauma on his own and with a never-ending social life. He called it social therapy, which included more than a fair amount of social drinking for a teen—beer and whatever was in the liquor cabinet of his friends' homes.

One of my most unusual observations about Mark was how he always had friends who stuck by him. He enjoyed lifelong friendships, while I've tried hard to forget my school peers and force them to stay locked in my past. Never in his life did Mom forbid a friendship of his. Not one of his friends entered her delusions and turned into psychopathic criminals that had to be cut off.

Mark pointed out that by the time he was eleven, Mom had already begun treatment, making him free to form meaningful and long-lasting relationships. Her regular psychotropic drug regimen, managed by Dad, quieted her mind. As a result, she happily drove Mark to his friends' houses in Upper Arlington, and his friends' parents brought him over to ours with no issues. The home on Winterset Drive was not a scary place for them. Throughout Mark's school years, his friends proved a powerful support system that Dalya and I had to do without.

Despite the few good memories with Mom, I could never predict when I would become her enemy again. One wrong move, and it was over. Repeatedly, reality plunged deep into what I now know is heartbreak. If I wasn't acting too much like Dad, I failed to submit to the delusional "don't talk to that person" or "call the police" orders. One minute I was her best friend to commiserate over evil, the next, her enemy to be thrown out indefinitely.

I begged God to help me remember. It was like searching for needles in a haystack. In my college days, Zak and Nan were youth leaders at church. Nan was like an older sister. She, like her love and faith, is a robust, happy memory. She invested in me with her care and time for four years. There were other mentors from other churches—genuine church servants that inspired me, like tireless Martha, always joyful, always making me feel like I belonged even though I wasn't regularly involved in her ministry. One of the teachers, Mr. Morrison, sticks out as being unusually kind during the horrific last year of high school. That was around the time Dad told me on the phone that I was pretty.

Playing my piano was an escape from life. Once, I played almost every Broadway tune in my Les Miserables book of music while Dalya sat beside me on the bench. We sang to my accompaniment, pausing between songs for me to explain to her the storyline. Once, she told me it was a good memory for her.

My eyes opened every morning to the sun streaming into my bedroom through the window situated on the upper half of the wall. I had a pretty white French provincial bedroom suite and my radio with a cassette player. My bedspread was covered with butterflies. My siblings and I used to catch fireflies at night in the backyard and watch them light up the pickle jar.

A few weeks after I gave her the bracelet while unpacking a housewares box she had returned to me for storing, I spotted the unwrapped box tossed in a glass pan, bracelet still inside. She had given it back. On the phone, she confirmed her intention of returning it. "Ceci, I don't wear this stuff," she said impatiently. It was gold with a dangling charm that etched a tiny flower bouquet and the word *Mom*. She was always buying similar gifts for us, including fashionable and fine jewelry, but never any good at receiving them.

She's not rejecting me, just the stupid bracelet, my head brooded. My bleeding heart muttered, goodbye, Mom. Just goodbye. The good times are long gone.

I was trying, but in the two years prior, I had been consumed with dealing with my past and the devastating emotions I had swept under the rug in my teens and twenties. They had snuck out and waged war on my mind, and I was fighting.

In the black of sleepless nights, smothering pain engulfed me. Seething words permeated my brain. "I want to die, and it's your fault." I dreamt of slapping her across the face with my words. But when I hold her face in my head, she gazes calmly at me. Only silence ensues.

The dream continues, and I rage on.

"I hate you."

"I never want to see your despicable face again."

"I'm sorry, I ever met you." (I was just warming up).

"For someone whom everyone loves so much, you're surprisingly hateful."

"You're smug, stubborn, and proud."

"If they only knew who you are."

I see her behind my eyes. No sound comes from her mouth, but her lips are moving. "How dare you talk to me like that?" Her question is predictable, justifiable, in response to my biting words. I'm ready with my comeback.

"How dare you ignore me."

"How dare you give birth to me only to manipulate me, abandon me, lie to me."

"Because of you, I curse the day I was born."

"I despise the day you were born."

The dream suspends, but my feelings don't. I had never hated her like this. It felt good to think these thoughts, despicable as they were. Ruby said that I couldn't have forgiven her back then. I needed first to realize what exactly I forgave her for. She donned another incredible realization on me—it was *okay* to say and feel these things, aloud if necessary, even if true that the pain experienced was a result of her illness. The fact that it was neither deliberate nor malicious did not forbid me from acknowledging its terrible effects on my family and me.

The stifling air was stuffed with the venom of anger and deep ache, one that has no words. In the black of a long night, I wanted to die. In that black, I called the suicide hotline for the first and last time. The soft-voiced man who answered my call was gentle and kind. His first comment was that it was good that I called.

Ruby blamed the Prozac, which was of no use. Mark and George willed me to stay active—even if it meant just going through the motions—and call the psychiatrist to try another antidepressant. Mollie said she needed to kick my rear end, but she used another word for that body part. I was glad. It lightened things a little. But Mollie could have said anything, and I'd cling to her words like a toddler grasps her mama's thigh. Growing up takes a painstakingly long time on the second try.

Loud, proud, opinionated, demanding, sarcastic, exhausting, complaining, untrusting, controlling, and never wrong, describes Mom. Lily is yet strong, courageous, intuitive, fun, flirtatious, engaging, resourceful, frivolous, independent, affectionate, and exciting. Thanks to Mollie, I *know* these things about Mom now, though I can't always see or feel them. I love her more than before, not out of obligation or by virtue of our bloodline. I love her for who she is.

I love her, though she shattered my heart without meaning to. Mollie, whom I love as well, also broke my heart without meaning to. To recover and stand on my own feet, I walked away from both—two of the hardest things I'd ever had to do.

CHAPTER 20

A Surprise Battle

Breast Cancer
2018

*Who is the man who desires life, and loves
many days, that he may see good?*
—*Psalm 34:12*

In Ohio's Octobers, the maples are their reddest and the ginkgos their yellowest. The splendor of the season steals my breath. My eyes savor the mellow sweetness as I drive the narrow country roads. My creative Anastasia, now sixteen years old, named her own scent for her soy candle at the Candle Lab "Golden Sweetness" as she mixed an oil blend of mulled cider, pomegranate, and autumn leaves. Years ago, to preserve the color of our backyard leaves for as long as possible, the girls and I dipped the brightest we could find into hot, melted beeswax and made garlands out of them with sewing thread. We draped the house with them.

How do I stop the color from fading?

Dad used to say that nothing in this world lasts. Every material thing, even in nature, has an end. The eternal things are not touchable with our hands, nor visible with our eyes. We can't hear with our ear's spirit-matter, which continues forever. But everything else comes and goes, just as the food in the fridge, the most elegant building construction, human life, and bright red maple leaves.

All the withering away of the world, including a body with cancer, didn't wither my hope and joy. It could have. Many people fighting cancer taste the day, month, or year-long bitterness of the loss of hope and joy. For some, hope and joy return.

There is a sublimely proficient explanation for the fact I was not crushed when the surgeon called the day after Thanksgiving of 2017 to confirm the tumor in my left breast was malignant. November must be my month of surprises. I was never sad too long during the long bouts of chemotherapy, physical pain, oh the headaches, and fatigue. I rarely felt lonely. I didn't ask why or raise my fist to the sky. It would have been understandable. Truthfully, it was an inside joke between God and me.

There are witnesses. I spoke the words into the air and unwittingly into His ears. *I'd rather have cancer.* I had repeated it to a handful of trusted friends for years. I'd take cancer over mental illness and all its misery. I wasn't serious, of course, but He took me up on it. And I'm not sorry.

Amazing how He makes me smile wide in the throes of pain. Astounding how He saved me from the affliction of fear with another affliction, how he distracted me from my worst fears by lending me a taste of someone else's, and so many others.

I was not scared of this four-and-a-half-inch mass that was growing fast. Last year's mammogram had come up clear as the Bahamian waters. Hadn't I already grieved loss much more significant than that of my hair? Hadn't I known fear? Hadn't I known severe pain and flirted with death just one year ago?

A lifetime of angst in childhood and motherhood and two years of my clinical depression prepared me. Family and close friends worried, but my heart had already withered like the maple leaves come November when they brown and swirl to the ground. Depression had me falling dizzy right up until it didn't have me anymore. Then cancer came, and, to be brutally honest, I laughed because the invisible part of my story begs to be told.

Pain is everywhere, in every corner and corridor, in the day's light and the night's night, sometimes visible, sometimes not. The suffering of humanity occurs before and behind the scales that obstruct vision.

The anguish on earth might not end, but it pauses inside of the lives of humans. It comes and goes, like Denise's Homemade Ice Cream in Clintonville, best parlor there ever was, friends, whistling cardinals, booming thunder, bad dreams, and autumn's colors.

The pause eluded me while going through depression. I couldn't see an end as I could with cancer. With Mom, there was no end in sight to the madness. Hence my proclamation that cancer is just not as awful because at least I knew one way or another, I would come to the end of it.

But it's different now. As I breathe in the autumn of the old year, I breathe in the old days. I'm no longer afraid to remember the suffering and the sparsely scattered good old days that are gone. The new normal of a trial is not so unique. I can have ongoing problems and pain without being consumed by them. Instead of working on my problems, I try to focus on working out my salvation, one of those invisible forever things. In Philippians 2:12-13 it says, "Therefore ... work out your own salvation with fear and trembling; for it is God who works in you both to will and to do for His good pleasure."

Isn't it a dazzling truth about Him and us? It is not my work, but *His* work *in* us so we can be lights in this dark world (vs. 15)—like the hundreds of summer fireflies that put on a light show every night along our creek out back. What if we could *allow* hurt, frustration, boredom, loss, loneliness, insecurity, and awkwardness to ebb and flow through days while the air of joy stays constant and we breathe *that*.

I want to shout this from every mountain now that I know it and claim it. Suffering is not a thing to escape but to embrace. (See 1 Peter 4:12-13.) I knew I wouldn't have to ask for help with cancer like I did with depression. A staggering outreach from everywhere pulled me into the bosoms of my family, church, homeschooling, and Zumba groups. George and I and the kids were immensely covered in everything good, and I was immersed in love, soft and loud.

If I could, I would dip all that love and care of the past and present into the beeswax. All those people were my red maple leaves. Right this minute, I would dip my children into the crockpot. They will not stay in the house forever. But stifling them in the house as we were during the quarantine would do nothing for their color.

I was even absorbed in wellness! By the time I finally made an appointment with the outstanding folks at Revive Chiropractic, Zumba Sis Michelle had all but deposited me in her car and taken me there herself. They placed me on a very low-carb diet, a heavy supplement regimen, and regular spinal adjustments. They didn't need to tell me to keep exercising. I was still going to Zumba classes and even teaching a little.

The seed had just been planted a few weeks before when, in cold, dreary March, we met John of Oakland Nursery, who was the designer scheduled to do a one-hour consult for our landscape. That providential appointment had turned into a two-hour workshop with George and me to cure cancer naturally. Standing next to my bare weeping cherry that had refused to bloom from our ground, this kind stranger shared details of his struggle with stage four colon-liver cancer and how, despite a six-month pink slip, he won.

For preventing and fighting cancer, the wellness protocols taught by Revive and the separate, unrelated personal testimony of our landscape architect closely matched. I'll never forget what John said as he sketched in ten minutes a practical and gorgeous blueprint for around the deck and backside of the house: "You have to decide whether you want to live or whether you want to die."

The concept of natural treatment was an enigma to us. Willing to entertain John's seemingly ludicrous idea of curing your own cancer, we began to study the foreign language of alternative medicine marked by holistic care. The more we learned, the more I was intrigued. The approach of proactively healing the mind, body, and spirit together with both eyes on prevention resonated with me. This mindset differs drastically from conventional medicine, which emphasizes treating the physiological symptoms more than addressing the possible causes of all three facets of our being, which are interwoven.

I found myself tiptoeing around the new ideas at the follow-ups with the cancer doctors, who remained an integral part of my care. I did not abandon the treatment plan but proceeded as scheduled with eight chemo treatments, lumpectomy, and six weeks of radiation. We blasted the thing. But after acutely irritating the oncologist with the information that I had eliminated sugar because it grows cancer cells, the decision was made to avoid the subject entirely from then on and focus on genuinely thanking him for his care in my case.

Meanwhile, my spinal adjustments and daily ingestion of a massive assortment of natural supplements boost my immunity and fight the toxicity of the chemo. Before my last infusion, I accompanied Anastasia and her violin group on a music tour in the Czech Republic. After resting the first day, I attended every performance and walked all over Prague, Ceske Budejovice, and the adorably quaint Cesky Krumlov with no issues. The doctor had conceded to help me get there by issuing a one-week delay of the white-blood-cell boosting Neulasta to avoid the ensuing vicious migraines.

Before all this, we were always told to do what the doctor says. The medical people know best. Trust the doctors; they are highly educated. They study the body more than anyone. So, it was with some trepidation that I decided not to do the five-to-ten-year hormone therapy drug, tamoxifen. "Why," Revive Owner Dr. Brandon Shriner asked, "work so hard to detox you only to put the toxins back in?"

My heart fell with another mammoth decision to make. It never occurred to us that we were being led down the wrong path. Being homeschool and Sunday School educators, George and I embrace knowledge from everywhere. And we didn't let go of God for a minute, not that we could even if we had tried. He always shows up when I need Him. Always:

Just cease to function except through Me. I am your Lord; obey Me... Just have no choice but mine, no will but mine. I am dependent on no one agency when I am your supply. Through many channels, My help and material flow can come.[1] —God Calling, March 20th.

Well, that takes care of that.

More little love notes from God appeared regularly on the right day, at the perfect moment. It was like He was texting me precisely when I needed it. And as if that wasn't enough, I was placed on the hearts, prayer chains, ropes, and lists of many warriors. They didn't have to tell me. I knew it on my knees. There were moments in the dark when I sensed an army behind me, ambushing my silent attacker with tears, pleas, and requests. Heal her, give her strength—comfort husband and children. If I could dip those colorful tears and prayers in my beeswax and keep them forever, I'd have to buy a lot of beeswax.

In October, almost one year after my diagnosis, the fuzzy grayish-black hair that sprouted from my scalp a few months ago has lengthened a little to the familiar curls I had missed. It is Breast Cancer Awareness Month. But inside this pink-ribbon campaign of fundraising and racing for a cure is a day for brain health—October 10th: World Mental Health Day.

So, I can't help but think of cancer *and* mental health. My life's stresses in the years before my diagnosis might have had something to do with that cancerous mass. Conversely, unknown growing cancer cells in my body might have caused my mental deterioration.

I have been made aware of both possibilities. So, which came first—depression or cancer? Will I ever know? Does it matter? Regardless of the order of things, human support and medical and natural treatments were integral parts of the healing process for my malignant mind *and* body. The point is empowerment. I was not a victim, but a fighter and survivor. As much as this teacher could be taught, the sleeping warrior inside me woke up and fought.

The invisible treatments of prayer and meditation helped remove stress-inducing fear and tension, which insidiously swell cancer cells. Ongoing stress and anxiety have the power to prevent us from coming to terms with overwhelming problems and rising above them—whatever the outcome. If the mind and body are inseparable, so are their healing.

The thought of Me is the salve for all sorrows. By thinking of Me and speaking to Me, you can always find healing for all physical, mental, and spiritual afflictions. Doubts and fears? Think of Me, talk to Me... sweet joy will flow. This never fails. Courage. Rejoice.[2] —*God Calling, October 8*[th].

If prayer is the foundation of all healing and all healing is ultimately divine in nature, then healing is the eternal thing, while suffering is just the lesson, the catalyst that draws us near to the great healer. Isn't that what He wants in the end? To bring us near *to Him* and to heal us? St. James exhorts, "...*pray for one another* that you may be healed." *James 5:16*

During depression and cancer, I was more aware than ever of invisible healing. The words that came to me in my devotionals, Scripture, prayer, and liturgy, soothed every tension and relieved the withering cells in my mind. The reliable relief kept hope alive and joy miraculously full. That joy fueled the strength needed in the hardest times, and when I looked up, it always came. Always. "Do not sorrow, for the joy of the Lord is your strength." Nehemiah 8:10

Faith is strength. Joy is strength. Joy heals! In Proverbs 17:22 we read, "A merry heart does good, like medicine, but a broken spirit dries the bones." When it's all you can do to *remember* that you can be strong in the fight when weakness seems like it *will* take over, *faith* and *trust* renew, and you don't fade away as the falling November leaves.

Staying the fight, you remain. And you overcome. Because though the body is not, your soul is forever. It's that part of you that cannot shrivel when it's filled with the other eternal, invisible things, like love, faith, and hope. These unseen medicines treat cancer and every other tiny and tumultuous thing in this hard world. They deepen your color.

Suffering in faith and joy is the beeswax that He dips us in to keep us close, bright, and colorful—like a maple leaf in autumn.

PART 4

Stir Up Love

CHAPTER 21

Reunions

When They Don't Want to
Talk About It
2018

*A 'hello again' after the final goodbye is sometimes
harder than just keeping the goodbye as it was.*
—*Jessiqua Wittman, A Memoir of Love*

When it rains, I'm a little melancholy in my room. The
rain clouds splash the window as my memories splash
the pages. During the happy summers, when we drove north
to visit my relatives, I was oblivious to the dreary future reality
that one day they would despise (or at least have nothing to
do with) my life's purpose of pulling my mother's mind out
of the darkness and lifting it high into the light.

Making people outside of the circle of my relatives aware
of Mom's brain condition captured the attention and harnessed
compassion. Friends and co-workers responded by doling out

refreshing, healing encouragement. Their words were more than comfort. They were a balm to my soul. Rarely did I sense the listener's uneasiness, but then I didn't start talking about mental illness until my thirties. George, my husband, knew all, but we did not discuss it with his family until fifteen years after we married.

When I began openly sharing our story, many other strange, exciting things were set in motion. That they were happening soundlessly inside the high walls around my entrails does not minimize their significance. I braved others' reactions. I discovered that my family was not abnormal. I realized that I possessed the freedom to be me. And there is no me without mental illness.

Because my mother's brain has a chemical imbalance, and I grew up watching and deciphering the confusing symptoms she displayed, I reacted by absorbing them and the stigma that followed. Next came shame, blame, and fear. Though it was not I who had the disease, I soaked much of its effects like a sponge soaked in vinegar and consequently suffered in other ways and had my battles to fight.

Ultimately, one of the effects of growing up with a parent with mental illness was deep sadness—of which I was not aware until twenty years after marriage and children. Navigating my sorrow led me to retrace my life's path back down that painstaking road toward little-girl me.

Speaking the truth out loud is not wrong, just painful at times. When I finally reached the bend in the brushy path that would be free of the thorns of secrets, fear, and shame, I was a river of peace and a lion. My roar had to blast somehow. I was an infant being reborn, pushing my way out into the vast open space. Through my brand new, sparkling, crystal clear, un-smudged lenses, I would see a whole new world. I would inhale a fresher, purer air. I chose to exhale on my blog.

Relatives whom I deemed close to me on deeper levels than the blood that flows in our veins had a different opinion. When I spoke up, misunderstandings erupted into "how could you" and "why did you." With some members, I did not have the opportunity to explain why I was opening up. I was never asked why; I was only criticized. Some of them cut me off. One publicly wrote that I am a *bad daughter*. Hot emotions ended in cold wars. My temper flared, and I claimed I didn't care—but I did. I didn't want to. I would have rather had the gall to stick it to them—those annoying people I love, whose faces drift through my consciousness and my dreams—the relations of my past, my mother's family.

Her five brothers and two sisters, both younger, were different hues of my mother's colors. Tante Ferialle and Tante Mervet were the silver and bronze to her gold. Their laughter, equal in pitch, and ease were as delicate as their sensibilities, as pretty as their classy clothes, as ready as a doorman awaiting your arrival. They were happily in love with their husbands. Mom was not.

They were always ready to hear my problems so they could commiserate and hear my good news so they could celebrate. Supreme Egyptian chefs each in their rite, they served up the best food. George still talks about Tante Ferialle's ribeye, grilled chicken drumsticks, zucchini bake with bechamel, and filo-wrapped choices of feta, spinach, or beef. The memory of Tante Mervat's kofta, pasta bakes, and cookies still make my mouth water.

Mom vehemently insisted that they were both better cooks than her. My siblings and I still shake our heads in disagreement. Nobody made a meatloaf like her. Her falafel, fresh and green on the inside, was fried to perfection and served with tomato salad, chopped with onion, fresh parsley, and cumin.

Mom inherited Gido's flare for salads: potato, beet, tomato, and cucumber discs arranged on a platter and dotted with a little oil, vinegar, and of course, salt. In another traditional mix, potato, parsley, garlic, and ground cumin with plenty of oil and vinegar was finished off with a pinch of cayenne. Even now, in her microwave oven at assisted living, she has figured out how to make the very stuffed grape leaves we grew up on!

Of all her brothers, Mom was closest to Uncle Nader. Perhaps they were the most alike in personality. Mom reeled with excitement when he came to visit. She bustled about frantically cleaning the house and cooking up food to feed an army. He loved her cooking. One, two, or three of the brothers would attack her hot chili pepper, tomato, and onion salad. The last two ingredients were the non-essentials. Food was important, and so was family. This is why we had reunions.

Toronto, the immigration landing for Mom and the entire Makar family, was our gathering locale. Everyone stayed at the quaint little old three-bedroom on Forman Avenue that belonged to our grandparents. Though it was not far from downtown, trips to the city were rare. The cousins played in the basement while the adults chatted upstairs in the family room. When she wasn't cooking and baking, Teta toggled between The Guiding Light and General Hospital on the box remote control and learned a fair amount of English.

Gido chain-smoked cigarettes and his pipe all day. His laugh was an uproarious cackle that was satisfying even without the knowledge of what exactly he was laughing about. He was a retired accountant whom I did not know that well. I've been told that he had been a dictatorial father back in Egypt. His children addressed him as Haadritahk, Sir. Mom addressed him as Papa, the way the French say it, with the accent on the second syllable.

Once, he wrote and mailed a letter to me—a short shower of grandfather blessings. The precious note is tucked away in my things, and, occasionally, I pull it out and re-read it.

I imagine him writing, choosing the words carefully and perfectly. His English was very good for a retired immigrant.

One thing was certain. He loved his grandchildren to the moon, and his love for Teta was deeper than the Mariana Trench, higher than Everest. I grew up hearing how much he loved her, but I didn't need to. If you were looking, you could see it plain as day.

Teta Therese was the glue and gleam of the family. To say she was special would not be fair. Special is sort of a vague word that can mean unique. She was unique in a thousand ways, and to everyone, she was marvelously so. To say she was a great cook would not be fair, but to say she was the greatest cook and cookie chef in all of Canada would do some justice.

She was kind beyond fairness. More merciful than just, she was yet wise. And you always felt loved—simply, faithfully, warmly. Her personality was warm, and her voice was soft, though I don't remember her sitting very much.

I do remember her scent. Once, a small candle at Anthropologie struck me with the matching aroma of her perfume that I didn't realize I had known intimately. I was transported back to her bedroom, where I used to sleep sometimes. I bought it and shuddered when all the wax was gone. Like she had gone away from me all over again. Teta died of lung cancer when I was thirteen.

We grew up knowing our cousins because of the reunions. All except one, the families made a point of gathering every other year. It was enough to sit around and talk from sunrise to sunset. The emotive talk was infused with non-stop jokes. When we were old enough to discuss life and things, the rich and cheeky conversations never failed to please. We never spoke of Mom's imprisoning viewpoints. No one ever mentioned anything about her strange beliefs and behavior. Uncle Boulos, Tante Ferialle, and their kids never came. No one ever talked about this missing family and their absence.

In my presence, it never came up. When I was little, I figured they were responding sensibly to the fact that they were bad while Mom and the rest of the family were good and that they cared little about reunions. This imaginary idea made me even more curious about them. Did they ever ask about Mom?

Tante Ferialle was Mom's sister. Would they ever see each other again? More than a decade had passed. What was she like? Was she like Mom? Did she laugh loud and clean the house every day and constantly worry about her children? Did she cry at sad movies? Did she watch the same soap operas Mom watched? Was she a light sleeper? Did she speak French like Mom? Did she tell her kids to eat before leaving the house? Did the rest of the family visit them?

In time, I would learn the answers to my questions. When I "met" Tante Ferialle again in late high school, my soul filled in a way that defies description—seeing her produced the same fulfillment as the black tea with sugar she made for me in her kitchen with the orange chairs and whimsical wallpaper. Warm, sweet, and comforting. She never skimped on the sugar or the size of the mug. Like hanging out in her kitchen, it was a treat to be savored for as long as possible.

All the family treasured the gatherings. Had English been their first language, it would not have been any easier to describe how much everyone loved to gather.

When I discovered as an older teen that the Makar family reunions were, in fact, every year, not every other, my world capsized. Uncle Boulos, Tante Ferialle, and cousins Nevine and Pete had been going in the off years. All this time, the extended family had also been gathering without us regularly. All this time, *we* were the odd ones out, not them. We were the black sheep. I imagined them laughing aloud and talking about us. I could hear the whispers about my mother that before I did not understand.

Inner shock waves solidified into walls. These walls were invisible to everyone, including me. Because the experience of feeling excluded is like magic ice that shoots the walls high into the sky. Those walls are not covered in pretty wallpaper.

CHAPTER 22

Raising Her Mind

The Effects of Stigma

Hope is the thing with feathers, that perches the soul,
and sings the tune without the words,
and never stops at all.
—Emily Dickinson

When reunion time approached, a special giddiness bubbled up, and the expectation of ongoing laughter was mostly brought on over summers in Toronto. Mom's brothers each had their own quirky humor that never failed to make us giggle or howl. Just waiting for the next sassy observation and ensuing retort among them was half the fun for me. Five minutes did not pass in the company without the effervescent chuckling of grownups and kids alike, Gido's superior roar towering overall.

Laughter makes you forget the pain. We were good at laughing together, and this indeed is good. It was the Makar way of bonding. And I needed that bond like a baby needs milk. Like food, it was crucial. It gave me a kind of strength, of which I was unaware. And that strength produced a sort of hope that lived in me somehow. Laughter invokes hope.

Reuniting with the Makar family hugged the chasmic parts of my heart tight because these jovial people knew me in ways no one else did. Pointing back to the same ancestors, we share a unique history. Connecting easily in the moment, we share the present. Knowing we will always have each other, we will always be family, we relish the future.

Better than food, our togetherness teleported us to our Egyptian roots — our parents' parents, their food, language, and inspiriting embrace. Besides being my identity, I relied on Mom's side of the family to give me that sense of belonging. That elusive thing that appears and disappears from Sunday school, Tante So-and-So's kitchen, ululation and belly dance at weddings, school classrooms, pep rally bleachers, football stadiums, and soccer fields that shaped me as an Egyptian and an American.

I, a hybrid of two cultures, am never completely either or both. How could I have known the ocean-deep extent to which I needed this attachment to my maternal members? The realization dawned when an uncle died recently, and they wordlessly turned their backs toward me at the church and remained speechless, rendering me the same on that sad day. My blog posts were too hard to swallow. Too revealing. Too painful. Too real.

Uncle Boulos' funeral provided closure for his death, which was badly needed. But the hot sting of stigma seethed right through my bones. This was the family of my childhood—an extension of myself. I believed that because I am also a Makar, they could never turn their backs on me. After all, love does not do that. Love, if it is modeled after Christ, does not fail. It is kind and patient, not easily angered. It protects, trusts, hopes, perseveres.

It seeks understanding. Since Dad passed on, we rarely heard from the relatives. My brother and I were not contacted to find out how she was doing and how we were doing for that matter. Except for Uncle Nader, Tante Mervet, and a couple of cousins in the last decade, throughout our life, no one reached out to discuss or ask questions about what happened to Mom's mental health and how it affected us.

Especially Dalya, who bore the brunt of her illness the hardest. My sister was too sensitive not to internalize the conflicts in our family, even when it wasn't about her. But soon enough, it would become about her.

Dad commented about this many times. He marveled and wondered why his wife's siblings so rarely expressed to him their concern for her and with such edgy tension when they did. Sometimes, allowing his thoughts to be heard, he said that they must not believe him. But in most conversations, he expressed sincere bewilderment. I always believed that they just didn't want to talk about it because it is too scary, sad, and ugly.

Little did we both know that they placed the blame squarely on him. I was told later by two of my mother's siblings that it was Dad's fault she got sick.

At the time of the recent funeral, immediately following their flagrant rejection of me, George, and Mark, no one spoke to us except cousin Dorothy, who has always been supportive and willing to listen and engage in the discussion about the mental illness in the family, a welcome relief for me. When she heard of the reaction to my post about Uncle Boulos, she called, and we talked.

My brain understood this incident as an affirmation of the fact that somebody in this family cares with sincerity, a thing wireless telephone waves can't hide. Add the pocket-sized sacrifice of taking the time to call me, a sprinkle of compassion and commitment to family, the humble act of reaching out, though we had not spoken in person in years, and you have a shining, albeit rare experience of family love enacted during conflict.

In 1 Corinthians 13:4-7 we feel the impact of this.

Love suffers long and is kind; love does not envy; love does not parade itself, is not puffed up; does not behave rudely, does not seek its own, is not provoked, thinks no evil; does not rejoice in iniquity, but rejoices in the truth; bears all things, believes all things, hopes all things, endures all things.

Notice how these words don't ignore a conflict in the area of love. It is conflict that rouses the need in the first place for patience and avoidance of envy, pride, anger, and sinful thoughts.

What if they had just asked the reason for my writing? What if they called or wrote with a question toward appreciating my purpose instead of sewing assumptions into the family tapestry, blackening it with division and slander? If they were upset with me, I was completely unaware until Uncle Boulos passed. Why didn't they reach out to their niece and seek clarity amid the confusion? Had I had the chance to explain, perhaps they would not have been so utterly shocked. They still might have disagreed, but they might have recognized one or two of my reasons and gained a small amount of understanding. Better than the chosen alternative.

I am far from perfect and hardly a great model of how to love. I think I was more of a minimalist family lover. Ever hesitant to initiate the conversation for fear of being met with apathy and rejection, I kept my mouth shut. This did not help. Fear never does. It only ensures that no window opens, no curtains are drawn even for a small peek into our lives. My silence and distance did nothing to narrow the gap and widen the view so they could understand. Contrarily, it widened the gap and narrowed the view.

All I ever wanted for the family was to understand. This would only be possible if they could see inside our daily lives. In recent years, with a significant nudge from Zumba, I became aware of a roar inside of me that needed to come out. Opening a little soul-window view would not be enough. Instinctively, I unbolted the colossal door to my heart, soul, and mind. In bits and pieces, I told all on my blog, *Come You Children*. And when I finally did throw open that door, instead of love on the other side, hate met me.

Well, that's how it felt anyway. While, again, I'm far from perfect in practicing love as described in Scripture, they treated Mark, George, and me with bitterness and disgust that day. Only a few spoke to us. The others would not even look at us. On that grievous funeral day, my brother and I had come seeking closure and comfort and the chance to console the mourners. Instead, we unwittingly walked right into a cold war that had not ended to the time of this writing.

My uncles, aunts, and cousins were their own bright window into Mom's soul, affirming her personality—the jovial, compassionate, high-strung Makar personality. Without them, there was no window. Their existence and presence in my life, especially at the gatherings, not only made me feel like part of a family but made me feel good about being Mom's daughter, even after her symptoms had escalated many times beyond everyone's control. They were the only extended family we ever knew. Dad's side is spread thin across three continents, and we did not know them. Except for one paternal aunt, Dalya, Mark, and I had never met a soul on the Raphael side.

Mom's side of the family offered me a small window into her background and good side, and I opened it. But the window I offered them, hoping they would get a clear view of our daily struggle with schizophrenia, was slammed shut.

"Every family has its secrets," an uncle scolded Mark and me at a cousin's wedding many years ago. "Some things are not supposed to be discussed." His gruff tone seized me. He was furious. Unwittingly, I had spilled the beans about Mom to his daughter Laura in a brief conversation at the reception. Mom's mood had escalated into a wreck of despair and agitation that night. Before all, her face was drenched with tears, agony spilling onto the pretty hotel reception dinner table covered in white linens.

She would not be comforted and concerned Laura had asked me why. Across the crowded party hall, I tried to explain, assuming she had known Mom was sick. I was dreadfully wrong. We were grown adults in our late twenties and thirties, and she had never learned that her maternal aunt had a severe mental illness. It was beyond my comprehension.

I was shocked and heartbroken. The new information had upset my cousin, but how could she have not known all those years? Who else didn't know? Or is the question who *did* know? Did any of Mom's nieces and nephews know their aunt had been diagnosed with schizophrenia more than a decade ago? It's a disease, not a criminal act. Why was everyone behaving as if it were the latter?

Stigma.

Weeks later, Tante Ferialle called me. "This is not the Ceci I know," she said. "Tell me you didn't mean to do this."

Do *what*? Am I a complete idiot to be so clueless as to my wrongdoing? Am I a deplorable, insensitive human? Mom had always criticized me for lacking empathy for others. Every time she did, the sting was a drill grinding into my temples. Inside, her words burned holes in me every time.

The family adored Lily, and Lily adored the family, except for her in-laws. But almost all my fourteen first cousins did not ask or speak about the condition of her mind until only the last ten years or so. And even then, a precious few showed a little interest. Once, Rasha and I stayed up most of the night talking about mental illness in our family. This meant the world to me. If any additional conversations between any other family members and I occurred that have escaped my memory, I am genuinely thankful. I wish there had been more.

Laura, not knowing, was a blatantly missing shriek of quiet despair. This is why we were alone. When the heart cries over a significant loss, the loss only swells and plunges to depths untold when locked inside a cave, or a glass room, or a castle made of ice—when you're not allowed to tell anyone.

Talking about it heals those who are afflicted by it. Then hope is birthed. I had learned *not* to talk, so I didn't, and no one talked about it with me. Rejecting me, the daughter of their sister, when I wrote about the mental disease in the family, is understandable, considering the culture, but still reveals the nasty effects of one word.

Stigma.

Even though my relatives on Lily's side were my entire familial experience growing up and I was a small part of theirs, and although they were my world in terms of family ties and toils, mental illness wreaked havoc on us all. When feared, it is, at best, a giant elephant in the room. At worst, it is a horrid monster that rears its ugly head frequently and unpredictably in the room, on the phone, in dreams of day and night. Amid fear, it divides and does not conquer. In truth, it seemed to conquer us.

Stigma is a stain that blights persons with mental disease and their loved ones, and the cost is immense. Mark, now a social worker and mental health leader, says it keeps people sick.

Severe mental illness like schizophrenia is not comfortable. In fact, it is excruciatingly uncomfortable. It makes the person in psychosis elusive, awkward, difficult to talk to, difficult to understand, unrestrained, abrasive, and cruel or at least seem so. It's hard to know what to say, and it's even harder to understand what they are saying. You can't calm them down. You can't erase the delusions or comfort them.

It is dismal because, like cancer, it doesn't go away if you ignore it. It only worsens. Mental disease is yet stubborn and sometimes feels very much like evil. It weakens your resolve because of its seeming hopelessness. You can't make it stop. By yourself, you can't do much.

Therefore, talking freely about it would have helped us monumentally, especially when we were young. If my immediate family had been allowed, stigma would not have been allowed to grow and emit its invisible but transfixing poison. Stigma is the monster's backside. No prettier, no less scary.

Stigma petrified our family, and it petrified me. Perhaps alongside schizophrenia, the surrounding social stain equally petrified Mom. I believe it prolonged treatment, discouraged the active pursuit of solutions for her and our family, and diminished hope.

Without stigma, her loved ones might have discovered ways to talk to her. They might have addressed her fictional ideas and fiery determination to pull stunts that we clambered to prevent. If she trusted us, we could have helped prevent her from calling the police on her brother-in-law.

I've thought about it a thousand times. What would have been a better reaction to mental illness in the family? And for that matter, outside the family? Perhaps STIR is one solution:

Speed up recovery
Talk about it
Instill hope
Remove stigma

These are my thoughts ardently strung around the words of the lustrous verses I learned long ago, like new lights weaved around the needles of a pine wreath, warm, bright, and fragrant.

And let us consider one another in order to stir up love and good works, not forsaking the assembling of ourselves together, as is the manner of some, but exhorting one another, and so much the more as you see the day approaching. Hebrews 10:24-25

Well, this four-part call is one way to *STIR* up love and good works. STIR in our family could have raised her mind from the pit of shame, blame, rejection, and isolation and covered it beautifully with the blanket of love, belonging, wellness, and hope.

CHAPTER 23

She Still Doesn't Know

What to do When They Have No Insight (Anosognosia)

"Whilst part of what we perceive comes through our senses from the object before us, another part (and it may be the larger part) always comes from our own mind."
—William James, *Principles of Psychology*

When I studied public relations at the university, a pervading theme of discourse was the notion that perception is truth. What you see, notwithstanding the lens through which you view it or the time or phase of your life when you consider it, is what is. After college, I worked for a homeless shelter. I knew that if people perceived homelessness, especially in women, they would be more likely to have increased compassion for them and donate as a result of mental illness. At the time of my employment, seventy-five percent of the clients in the women's shelter had a severe mental illness.

As a P.R. professional, I banked on this definition of truth. All decisions about communications with potential donors and volunteers were based on this motto. My goal was to change the perception about homeless people—that the responsibility of improving their circumstances lay more on the community and society at large than on the client.

Using facts and real stories evoking emotion about discrimination, mental illness, uncooperative laws, and stigma, I aimed to draw the attention toward the "big picture" of homelessness and what, therefore, we need to do about it. That was my job, regardless of my personal views, which had not been formed by the time I was twenty-two. Many times, it worked. People felt compassion and gave their time, money, and possessions.

But it didn't work with Mom. No matter how I tried, no matter how I cried, I could not change her perception. Despite the facts displayed before her and the emotions that spilled out of me, she would not budge in her thinking.

I challenged her thoughts with trepidation. Under a perceived threat of her permanent disapproval of me, I pressed, again and again, the ideas she must believe as real for her good and everyone else. I slid them into conversations, hoping to sneak them in. I was as subtle as the quills of a porcupine. She always knew.

"Stop saying nice things about Mona. They are lies. You are a liar."

"I'm not lying," I say with gritted teeth. "I want you to see her from a different view, from my view."

"Your view is wrong because you've been brainwashed by evil—by that evil girl and her father."

On my wedding day, five years later, Mona would appear and position herself discreetly in the back of the church. Though invited, she would skip the reception to avoid chaos. Her parents, who were like my second parents, our beloved Selim and Renee, would not attend. Their absence would be like a funeral to me and likely to Dad.

Multiple layers of accumulated resentment in me were the result of Mom's apparent refusal to entertain the idea that she might be having difficulty perceiving things as they are. The reason for this bitterness is that I viewed her reaction as sheer stubbornness and simple denial. Moreover, this unwillingness to even try to see things our way had resulted in social awkwardness and significant loss.

Dad said that you couldn't blame Mom, only the illness, for her attitude or behavior. While he made this look easy by the quiet way he bore his cross, it was not. It was painfully difficult for me.

My internalized indignation fairly evaporated only a year ago when I discovered a condition closely associated with schizophrenia. Upon reading, I learned that Mom was not rejecting our views or making up stories. She lacked insight into her skewed perceptions. This inability of the brain to perceive some areas of reality, including her illness, means that she does not make a conscious choice to disagree with us.

The Diagnostic and Statistical Manual of Mental Disorders[1] (DSM) is the authority on mental illnesses. Created and published by the American Psychiatric Association, this comprehensive reference describes all known mental disorders, including schizophrenia. Mental health professionals refer to it when determining the mental condition a person is experiencing. According to the DSM, "A majority of individuals with schizophrenia have poor insight regarding the fact that they have a psychotic illness. Evidence suggests that poor insight is a manifestation of the illness itself rather than a coping strategy... comparable to the lack of awareness of neurological deficits seen in stroke, termed anosognosia."[2]

I did not first learn of anosognosia in the DSM. I stumbled on it while reading a personal account in *I am Not Sick I Don't Need Help!* by Dr. Xavier Amador, a psychologist who researched the condition extensively. He tells the story of his older brother, who developed schizophrenia. "The research... that links poor insight to structural brain abnormalities leads us to only one conclusion. In most patients with schizophrenia and related psychotic disorders, deficits in insight, and resulting non-adherence to treatment stem from a broken brain rather than stubbornness or denial."[3]

It is not denial or stubbornness, as we thought. It is a brain dysfunction resulting in a lack of awareness caused by a change in the frontal lobe, which inhibits its ability to update and therefore reshapes the self-image. The brain's reshaping of the self-image is a constant process. In cases of chemical alterations, the person loses the ability to accept new information and renew their self-perception and the way they view their health. Simply stated, Mom's perception of herself and her mental health is stuck in a sort of time-warp. This makes her unaware and unable to accept her condition.

Understanding this unfortunate facet of schizophrenia made it much easier to accept Mom's lack of insight. Among people who suffer from the illness, fifty-seven to ninety-eight percent show signs of anosognosia.[4] Despite its commonness, there is no cure, only hope for an increased focus of research in that area. That a brain alteration might cause her lack of insight as opposed to stubbornness or denial makes it easier to swallow. Had this been on our radar as even a mere possibility, we might have taken a very different approach.

Arguing with a person with no insight into her illness, as I always did, does not move them any closer to receiving treatment. Attempting to refute their statements only worsens the situation by weakening their trust and isolating them more than ever. In his book, Amador discusses an effective method for gaining the trust of a loved one and helping them agree to take medication.

Research of anosognosia surfaced about one hundred years ago and revealed that it is a symptom of schizophrenia (and other diseases) and not a coping strategy like denial. Amador offers LEAP, a practical communication tool to engage consumers who lack insight and do not accept treatment.

- **Listen**: Without commenting or arguing, listen to him or her, then reflect aloud your understanding of what they said in your own words.

- **Empathize**: Express empathy with the reasons he or she has for not agreeing to accept treatment, even if they are unrealistic or ludicrous. This is not the same as acknowledging or admitting that their belief is true.

- **Agree**: Find and point out the facts on which you both can agree. Even when it seems you are completely opposed in every way; it is possible to find some point of agreement. This tool neutralizes your position with your loved one by making observations. For example, the question of what happened after the medicine was stopped might reveal they might not sleep well and start to feel worried or scared. Without connecting the medicine to having a mental illness, you can agree that a motivation to accept treatment might be to sleep better and feel less afraid.

- **Partner**: Partner to meet shared goals. Focus on the areas you agree, like staying out of the hospital, getting a job, etc., and working toward achieving them.

LEAP helps family members and mental health professionals to look beneath the symptoms to see the person—a beautiful concept. My heart winces as I try to recall if I ever really did that. Perhaps I accidentally practiced bits and pieces of this approach. Indeed, I listened to the long rants stemming from her delusions, expressed a half-hearted understanding of her feelings, and attempted to get her to agree to disagree. Sadly, I believe my uninformed, desperate responses did nothing to gain her trust and improve our relationship.

I wish my family had been armed with this method thirty-five years ago. The frustrations of deteriorated trust and never-ending battles about reality could have been prevented or lessened if we knew about anosognosia and Amador's method of response. But because LEAP had not yet been around, it was not God's will for us to know at the time. But it is available now, and it could be a valuable tool for the loved ones of mentally ill people.

Schizophrenia and undoubtedly, many other severe mental illnesses harbor a state of loneliness. The disease itself should not wholly be blamed. The surrounding stigma magnifies the feeling and reality of being alone in the fog and distress. Imagine being surrounded by this loneliness perpetually.

Now, further imagine the people closest to you—a mother, son, spouse, or friend—telling you that you're sick and demanding that you do something about it when you're not ill, that is, when you are sure that you are just fine and everyone else is crazy for thinking you're sick! This yields even more loneliness. Mom knew that the people closest to her believed she was ill. According to Dad, her siblings were highly apprehensive of venturing to offer the slightest, most gentle suggestion that she might be wrong about something or that a pill might help things for fear of crushing her. For years, I had the same concern.

LEAP is a grace-filled glide into the soul of a person living with a severe mental illness. While not necessarily easy, it is sensitive and captures their sensibilities. It opens the door and opens the heart. A graceful dancer leaps across the stage to beautiful music, engaging the viewer, drawing them in. This is what I wish I could have done a long time ago with Mom: LEAP into her *person* and draw her in, remove the isolation and loneliness, and make her come alive.

Now I know. Maybe she still doesn't know the common reality as it pertains to her life, but with a tool like LEAP, I know something to do to make progress and make things a little better for us.

CHAPTER 24

Was I Just A Passer-By?

Dalya
2020

There may be a great fire in our soul,
yet no one ever comes to warm himself at it,
and the passers-by see only a wisp of smoke.
—Vincent van Gogh

At the beginning of a new decade, unassuming humans everywhere stretched their eyes over the horizon of time and foresaw new opportunities and second chances, hopes, and dreams realized.

March arrived, and I wanted to reset the year. Like a computer with a virus, 2020 appeared to be highly infected. The onslaught of disasters combining a locust plague in East Africa, bushfires in Australia, a volcano eruption in the Philippines, plane-crash deaths of NBA star Kobe Bryant and his daughter, and a tornado outbreak just south of us in Tennessee, didn't scratch the surface. A fast-spreading virus, which causes a highly contagious airborne respiratory sickness, prompted the world to shut down.

With thousands dying and no vaccine, entire countries, including the United States, declared a state of emergency and told everyone to stay home. Schools, banks, gyms, hair salons, clothing stores, and restaurants closed (except for takeout). Employees and students worked from home. Life abruptly and dramatically changed.

The grocery stores remained open, but the toilet paper shelves turned up vacant every time we checked. As Americans purchased inordinate amounts of the bathroom staple, it became the weightiest panic-buy and a prolific subject of Twitter and TikTok posts to cut through mounting pandemic anxiety. Back in the day, we strung rolls of it all over the trees and houses of unsuspecting high school classmates for practical jokes! Today, the cheapest I could find on Amazon is 18-roll packs of an unknown brand for $29.99. The household Scott brand is unavailable. Charmin is nowhere to be found.

Are you kidding?

Never-ending April followed, and Americans stayed home to stay alive. Everything canceled, including the summer Olympics, high school and college graduations, and Anastasia's breathtaking music study-abroad in Switzerland. She had never been so excited about anything in her sixteen years. She would have been there on her birthday with her violin, her ensemble peers, and a few of the world's esteemed teachers rehearsing and performing in the Alps. How does a mama temper the blow of that closed door for a girl whose ultimate dream is to travel the world?

Juliana's college classes moved online so that my extrovert daughter was stuck at home, and I was secretly happy to have her at dinner again. Gabriel's basketball awards banquet and entire track season were erased. At the same time, to his utter chagrin, piano lessons continued through Zoom, an online meeting room, which was also used for Amelia's dance and my Zumba classes. Camp Kesem, an out-of-this-world week in the woods for children of cancer victims and survivors (and the only overnight summer camp we ever permitted), was canceled for 2020. Gabriel and Amelia had returned beaming last year. "It was the best week of my whole life," they caroled in one line of a glad melody and a thousand sparkling memories.

"Social distancing" is the primary preventative tool adopted by countries as we ride the wave of this pandemic. At the time of this writing, the medical people report that we are slowly sliding the peak. Lockdowns continue to be enforced. Humans are to keep six feet distance and no more than ten people in a space, even outside.

We are advised to meet "virtually" through online platforms, drink hot liquids with lemon, spend time in the sunshine, order takeout, and wear a surgical or cloth face mask in any public place if we must go.

The days run together. Sunday is practically indistinguishable from Wednesday, for even the doors of the church are closed. But the restrictions imposed on hospital visitors will pierce callously through our hearts and the black of April 3, a day that does not blend with the others.

It was Friday. Dalya's son, Dawood, found her unconscious on the floor of her bedroom and called the ambulance. On the way to the hospital, she coded, and it took the medics thirty-five minutes to bring her back to life. Thanks to the blasted quarantine, we were not allowed admittance to her room. They suspected the pervasive virus. After forty-eight hours of waiting, the test returned negative, and she was moved to a different ICU floor. Thankfully, a ventilator was available. Then suicide was suspected when her antipsychotic medicine bottles were found on the nightstand.

Please, God. Not this way.

God answered my prayer. A pulmonary embolism caused the collapse. Blood clots in her lungs blocked oxygen to the brain, which caused it to swell. The damage was irreversible. Meds could only help her breathe and make her comfortable until she passed. There was little they could do. The doctor said there was no sign of overdose.

Alone in the hospital room, we were told that we would be permitted to visit one time to say goodbye. The neurologist explained that one centimeter of her brain was functioning. Injured were all the parts that made her who she was. She will never be aware of your presence. "You must consider what she would want," the doctor said mostly to Dawood.

The hushed floors of Mount Carmel East appeared like ghost towns as if there were no sick people in a metro area of more than two million. At our first visit, the staff at the front desk ignored the pandemic policy of a maximum two at a time and allowed us to go to the room. Mom, Mark, Penelope, Dawood, Tara, and I all sat with Dalya as she breathed with her eyes half-open, not really there.

The next day her eyes were closed entirely. Dawood choked through tears that he still hoped for a miracle. Mom repeated it incessantly. "Jesus raised Lazarus. He'll raise Dalya," she said with force and passion. Then she looked at Dalya, and her tone switched in the still room on the hospital floor they called "end of life." With soft raised cords, she coaxed, "Wake up, Dalya, Habibty. Wake up."

A week later, still breathing by the ventilator, the doctor called. We had two days to decide. Remove her from the machine and let her pass naturally or have a tracheotomy, an incision in her neck through which a tube would be inserted to help her breathe. It is a gruesome long-term option that would keep her in a vegetative state indefinitely.

Dawood and his sister Tara, twenty and seventeen, wavered between trusting Mark and me because their mother for years portrayed us as untrustworthy. Mark sat down with Dawood that evening and talked.

Mollie texted. She heard from Ale about Dalya. When I saw the text, I remembered the detached blow I felt when she first told me about her younger sister, whom she had to let go a decade before as she was dying from muscular dystrophy. Once again, my friend, who is not a heavenly power, showed up like an angel. Knowing this kind of pain firstly with her sister and secondly with her patients, she drew a detailed picture of life with Dalya as a vegetable. It wasn't pretty. We all knew she would detest that option. Who wouldn't?

Five hours later, Mark called. He and Dawood had discussed the doctor's recommendation and had made the decision. Let her go.

Dalya grew up reserved and trapped. Everyone was always teasing her about her pace. She moved slowly about her days. She took her time in everything. Dad said she prayed before every bite.

Caught in the throes of our mother's mental illness, she drastically changed in high school. Along with switching from private to public, *she* switched from quiet to loud, from passive to downright defiant, and we began to wonder which direction her life would take. Her contagious laugh and passionate opinions about what was wrong and right with the world made life interesting—until she ran away and over time switched from victor to victim.

Where do I begin her story? With rebellion? To recount her adult life in detail would sound like a rerun of Mom's life.

I lost my sister way before she died. The winds of defiance turned into storms of paranoia, and I was pushed away by both. We all were.

Sometime during the transition to adulthood, she had begun to blow everything out of proportion. It was a mistake to chide her for being too sensitive. She never let us forget that. There was the time I crossed my legs while sitting on the living room couch at Mom's. We were grown women, and I was wearing baggy beige pants. She accused me of purposely flaunting my body in front of her, knowing how she felt about hers. My brain felt nails grating a chalkboard.

"You were never a sister to me," she said. When I told Mom, her words were just as scratchy as Dalya's. "No, you shouldn't have done that in front of her if it bothers her." From that day on, I was careful never to cross my legs in her presence.

It wasn't for lack of trying on both ends of the telephone wire. I forgot that George and our two older girls could hear me in the basement of our echoey Clintonville house as I shrieked into the receiver, begging her to believe me that I wasn't trying to hurt her, that I struggle with body image, and I'd never, ever flaunt it. She was not a black sheep, but a beautiful lamb in God's flock whom God loved infinitely, and why don't you ever believe me? George, startled by the sheer volume of my voice, hurried Juliana and Anastasia to the top floor to spare them the drama and prevent the typical Raphael screaming matches from becoming their disquieting normal.

Her nails might as well have scraped my chalky heart. I've always wanted to be close. I've loved her and been in awe of her. How did she so easily talk to everyone? What did she say? She was the skinny, pretty one. I was the overweight frumpy sister who couldn't clean up half as sharp. Where did I go wrong? How did I hurt her so? When did she fall apart? And how did we miss it? I am the worst sister ever, but I don't have a clue why. What happened to quiet, happy Dalya, who walked on her toes when she was tiny?

Dawood and Tara reported that Dalya had been motionless in bed for several months with depression before the day she collapsed. Then one day, she emerged from her room. For three days, she bustled about cooking and cleaning, apologizing for being a bad mother. The doctor concluded that several months of minimal movement in bed, then a sudden flurry of non-stop activity pushed the blood clots that had formed in her legs to the lungs and blocked the oxygen to her brain.

One night during this period, she was found by the police at four in the morning walking a busy street barefoot. This was not the first occurrence of night wanderings. They took her to the hospital from where she was discharged a few hours later. She explained that she had been assaulted.

Later that day, she told Dawood that she had made up the story. The real reason for roaming the dark road was that she had been seeking atonement from God and asking forgiveness for the burden she had been on others. I had only heard that kind of clarity one other time.

By the time we moved back to Columbus from Savannah in 2004, cousins Juliana and Dawood were preschoolers. They played in Mom's backyard while Anastasia and Tara drank apple juice from their sippy cups. As the years passed, time spent with Dalya diminished to never. Mom bought her a posh house in suburbia—$500,000 cash. She slowly gained weight and lost jobs and the house, which had deteriorated. She and her children isolated, never answering my calls or the front door when we knocked. She said she was homeschooling but spent days and nights in her room while the kids watched television. The neglect, induced by psychotic delusions, led to her rock bottom when she lost custody to Franklin County Children's Services.

You can only go up from rock bottom, so Dalya obeyed authority for the first time since the ninth grade. Her only aim was to retrieve her children. After one year of consistently working and taking antipsychotic drugs, she did just that. Then, I was told that during her inpatient rehab, she was diagnosed with paranoid schizophrenia. This was when I began to mourn for Dalya—sixteen years before her death.

I hadn't spoken about her. All those years, I was trying to protect her. I was trying not to make friends uncomfortable. How could I talk of Dalya without mentioning her diagnosis? I didn't reveal the slow rises and steep plunges to rock bottom that followed, not that they were new for her. I didn't blame a single soul, and I didn't make excuses. I did get angry, very angry. But I didn't talk about that either. I didn't say the way it was before diagnosis.

The signs. The accusations—how she ran away from home when she was a teenager. How I prayed all night long that she wouldn't get pregnant while unmarried, yet, she came back home with not one but two babies with two fathers, both non-existent. How she swore she wouldn't be there at Thanksgivings and my heart sank to the bottom of the Atlantic. I blocked the echo of Dad's haunting words weeks before he died in 2004. "I think Dalya is going down the path of your mom."

Funeral arrangements mingled with the investigation of Dalya's estate and plans for Dawood and Tara. She died on Orthodox Good Friday in the evening. The funeral was delayed, thanks to the pandemic. Cemeteries limited the number of burials per day, so there were fewer bookings. No one except the survivors could attend the service or approach the gravesite, where our priest conducted a brief prayer service. Mom refused to go. "There will be no funeral," said she. "Come back and get me when she's up and talking with you again."

I was angry. How are you getting away with this? I silently screamed at my dead sister, hoping she could hear me. You never kept a job, paid your property tax, mowed the lawn, went to the doctor, ate healthy, stayed on your meds, called me, allowed our kids to grow up together. As if I didn't know she had two of the biggest excuses on the planet—depression, and schizophrenia. At the moment, I didn't care.

Later, I would refuse to shout at her gravestone, forfeiting the usual silent treatment I had received from her countless times. Dawood informed us that she had requested to be buried in white clothes and that we all wear white at the funeral.

I remember her jokes—how she teased me. Teaching her the songs to Les Mis at the piano was one of the precious few meaningful moments we had together. She was quiet as a little girl but laughed loud and hearty as an adult. She argued and questioned everything. Her sense of justice was sharper than rose thorns and sometimes felt like them. I'm five years older, but there's so much I don't remember. The three of us siblings locked up for a time in the school of hard knocks, and her kids had received automatic enrollment upon their births.

I thought that eventually, we would overcome our issues and draw close to each other. We certainly had much to commiserate over. We also shared parents, faith, a love for home

176

decorating, mothering, and homeschooling. On the phone, our voices were indistinguishable, even to Mom.

But she was always rejecting me like oil rejects water—blistering accusations.

"You made me a scapegoat."

"You don't understand me."

"You just never will."

"This is all your fault."

"My whole life is your fault."

I wanted to love her. She seemed to want to hate me. She didn't. She couldn't even see me. And I could barely see her, only her jabs.

When she finally started taking meds, she appeared at birthday parties and one or two Christmas dinners. She was pleasant but distant, different than we knew her to be. It was like the drugs gave her back to us but took away some of her personality. She was subdued. I was grateful. Once, while I was briefly mentioning how much I used to worry about her, she responded, "You did? I'm so sorry. I'm so sorry I was such a burden." This rare clarity baffled me.

The emotional shoving was over—until she stopped taking the meds a few years later. Then she was gone again. Later, we would learn from her kids that the delusions remained active. She had acted congenial while telling Dawood and Tara that Mark and I were evil. As the effects of the meds diminished, she distanced herself more and more. The official social distancing spurred by the global quarantine had nothing on her. Days before her collapse, after her conversation with God, Dalya told her kids that it was okay to see us again. More clarity just before her final day on earth.

The morning of Good Friday, I awoke with a strong sense that she would die that day, so I drove to the hospital one more time, stood by her bed, and spoke through my mask. "You did a great job with the kids. Don't worry, we'll take good care of them."

The absence of sound in the room comforted my mind. It was just the two of us. I couldn't remember the last time Dalya and I were alone together. We hadn't seen her in at least two years. But for the first time in fourteen days since she fell unconscious, I felt a deep peace, as if in this room, He had led my soul to still waters.

"Did you know it's Good Friday?" I asked her. "Yes, it is. I love you very much, Dalya. I always have. I hope you can hear me, little sis."

I took her soft round hand in mine and held it for a minute because, for once, she couldn't stop me.

"Bye, Dalya," I said and walked out of the hospital. Mark called around ten that night. She was gone.

She loved bright colors. Red and turquoise couch pillows. Deep plum chairs. Dangly earrings with jewel tones. When she rented our brother's apartment for a time, she painted the ceiling dark brown, and the walls cream or pumpkin. I can't remember which. She lit torchiere floor lamps with the light facing up, and the room glowed.

She glowed. She was always making us laugh. And she detested injustice and vehemently expressed support or opposition to every issue. There was never a middle ground. She talked to everyone, and she could get anyone talking. She could draw and paint like an artist but snapped at me hard whenever I'd call her one. She was the most direct person I ever knew. "If you're not going to be forthright with me, forget it," she said.

Dalya was a fire in a cave that the world slowly extinguished. I crumbled, thinking I passed by cognizant only of a wisp of smoke.

I am broken for her and Mom. I am broken for the rest of us—two I loved trapped in their own minds. I couldn't get inside, and they couldn't get out. I can't break in and smooth my hand over their broken brains. She hated the sight of me as if I was her enemy. But a little medicine here, a little dose there, and she would have come back to me. We would have been friends again and talked about what is right and wrong with the world. She would smile at me with her pretty smile, one that is becoming a faded memory—one that looks a little like mine.

"Today, she's one day closer to dying," I wrote a few weeks ago as she lay unconscious in the hospital. Today, it is me who is one day closer to dying and seeing her smile again.

Was her death the real tragedy? Or was it that she did not know how much she was loved? Will she ever know? A friend assured me that somewhere deep inside of her, she'll know. We are so afraid of death. Its finality makes us crazy with worry. The memories and regrets rise over our minds like a tsunami, and we run from it. Death is an end, we think. Not Dalya. Her madness did not bar the clarity of a magnificent afterlife. Bible verses were found written and embellished in multiple journals. One of her favorite songs was *I Can Only Imagine*, by MercyMe. She had even planned the colors of her funeral—white.

May 29, 1987—I was fifteen when I wrote this poem about Dalya. She was ten.

Sister

I see a child
She stands there
No one's around
In her eyes, I see innocence
Her whole face says
I'm looking to be found.
I wish I knew her,
I mean really knew her
See right now what she'll become
What her face will say later

Baby was a princess
Always, she'll be
I see loneliness from the way she stands,
A thing she's just discovered.
Poor princess.
I see a child
She stays quiet if she wants
Or she stays wild.
Show me a thing more beautiful.
You can't.
This beauty is part of me.

CHAPTER 25

Loving Her Mind

Letting in the Light
February

I am not where you left me. I am in a better place.
Now I can come back to you.
—Written by the author

In the dark of 6 p.m., I feel the cold February air on my face and am secretly happy for the shorter days, as if the winter sun, turning in early, permits me to hide away from the world for four hours before bedtime. Putting on my homey, Mr. Roger's cardigan and slippers, I have been gifted time to snuggle with my youngest, Amelia, or read my current book.

This is Mom's birthday month. In the past few years, we have not celebrated. She doesn't want a party. She just wants to see us. She stopped dying her hair, and now it's white. Her face doesn't look that old for 77. The color is deliberate, different, pretty on her light skin, and dark brown eyes.

Her smile is ever deliberate. If she doesn't have something to smile about, she won't. So when she peers at you and smiles, be sure it's for you. Formidable, considering the evil that continually surrounds her and her children. For Mom, the committee of OSU psychiatrists has always existed in her life. In her mind, they are here to stay.

For the past thirty-five years of Mom's life, it has been difficult to speak of her without speaking of her mental illness. Even with Dad, discussions centered around her care or riding the continuous learning curve of how to respond to her comments stemming from her distorted thoughts. What do you say when she asks, "Do you believe me now?"

Dad's thinking was that answering affirmatively just fed her delusional thinking. Responding negatively to her hurts her feelings and weakens the trust between us, even when she is taking her medicines, and the hallucinations are quieter. Dad was so patient with her.

I wish we had known about the findings and methods in Amador's book a long time ago. We needed them badly. I devour its simple, elegant ideas for caring for a loved one who has little or no insight. They don't believe anything is wrong with their thinking. Their delusions are their reality. What if everyone told you the sky is red when you know it is blue? Welcome to Mom's world, and the world of about one percent of the global population that suffers from schizophrenia.[1]

For a time, I didn't want to try to love her mind. I didn't want anything to do with it or with mental illness. Can a daughter separate her mother's afflicted brain from her heart? Maybe then she could broaden the view. I wanted to perform surgery though I'm not a doctor. I wanted to sever the two, so I could extract the sickness from her and see her and discover her.

Mollie, whose brain is not chemically imbalanced, did that for me. Mesmerizingly similar to Lily, the lively Mollie, the figment of my childhood, personified my petrified mother. When we hugged goodbye one day as I was leaving Mom's room, her hand brushed mine, and the old familiarity swarmed. Instantly, I was back at the Orlando hotel three years ago, hand chained to Mollie's trying to stay, and even further back at the mall as a toddler, trying to run away. Since my friend held my hand and sprang me to life, I have wanted to grasp hold of Mom's and do the same.

Lily has a brain disease. She is mentally sick and always will be. Once, I said it out loud to a friend. When I finally allowed my voice to spray it into the air, I realized I hadn't poisoned it but had perfumed it with the truth that freed me from the chains of shame. I was not ashamed of her anymore.

When I could finally see more of her than her delusions and outbursts, I could rejoice over her as a precious creation of God with a beautiful mind, broken as it is. The broken vessels leave open the cracks to let the light in. That's how love then finds a way in.

Instead of falsely hoping she'd snap out of it or be healed just because I want it so, I accepted her as she is.

I could love her without wishing for a different kind of mother. Throughout a multitude of spells, I didn't have a mother at all by my estimation. I mourned as if I had lost her, though she was alive. Amador explains this as beneficial.

The research is clear on the importance of mourning. By mourning what has been lost, you open your eyes to all that is still there. Moreover, you open your eyes and heart to new possibilities ... Families that successfully mourn are able to let go of their anger at their loved ones. They learn to separate the illness from the person. Communication gets healthier, and even the course of illness can improve because of the lessened tensions between family members.[2]

That I no longer mourn what might have been is a great deliverance. I have found and kept a new hope—the hope of healing. A dream that a calmer, faith-strong outlook could set its sights on Mom as a spectacular human being, whose layers are many and profound, who loves her children and grandchildren, who have limitations, like the rest of us.

Lily—beautiful and fearless, strong and sassy, affectionate and bossy, and proud—knows what to say and when to say it. She even knows how to say it. She is stubborn and always right. Always. But when she smiles at you, bask in it. Her smile is warm and glorious and is especially for you. Have one conversation with her, the very first one, and you are smitten. By the time she is done with you, you feel lighter and prettier and a little wonderful. This is my mother.

Once upon a time, we could talk for hours. But now, we wrap our conversations around moments, whose memory will outlast the long days and years of rants about the invisible enemy in her chemically imbalanced mind. Today's moments count much more than hours of one-sided dialogue. Not because she has discovered a more accurate reality—she hasn't— but because I have found a way to love her without expectations.

I have learned to love her in and out of delusion. To love her whether or not I feel loved by her, and to love her on the days she's not speaking to me because I slipped and said, "mental illness." I love her when she won't be loved, when she won't receive care, when she doesn't care for me. Maybe I can't hold her hand, but I can hold her close with patience, forgiveness, and laughter, one of her favorite languages.

If she always fluctuates between clarity and fog, it's okay. She is not her illness though her diseased mind will not likely change. I learned to love it anyway because I'm not afraid or ashamed of it. And I'm not ashamed of her because I love her.

Ohio winters are long and dreary. Until spring comes, my houseplants will get more attention. I will savor the hot cocoa that will be forgotten in May. I will delight in Gabriel's basketball games, my cozy wool hat that I knitted years ago, and my books. What else can be done except count the February blessings that come unexpectedly? Slightly later sunsets, red roses, chocolate, and love that stretches far beyond Valentine's Day.

Love as warm as Mom's smile and as certain as my hands around her heart.

CHAPTER 26

Loving My Mind

These are the Good Old Days
2020

*They looked to Him and were radiant,
and their faces were not ashamed*
—Psalm 34:5

How are days with Mom now? The good exceed the bad if she is taking her medicine. It depends on our most recent conversation, the look in her eyes when we meet, the measure of pleasantness in her voice on the phone. Sometimes she is suspicious or upset, but sometimes she can draw close to me. Sometimes she can hear what I'm *really* saying, and sometimes she cannot. Under an array of various circumstances, the same could be said for everyone.

She visits with the grandchildren and enjoys viewing their latest photos on my cell phone. Shopping sprees at the mall with the change of seasons are followed by Cajun chicken or Subway. She still cooks for us.

A child growing up with paranoia as the language and force of reason will spend some years in a fog of fear, confusion, guilt, and shame. I don't know exactly when I figured out that I don't have to be ashamed of myself. Ruby pushed me in the right direction, and my new therapist continues to do so. But I do know that there were many years like that. My sky was not a changing, endless window into outer space. It was a ceiling with no holes, no air. Mom was there but not there. Dad was soberly trying to survive. There was no other family around. I lost every best girlfriend. I was kicked aside, embarrassed, ostracized. My walls flew up. Already awkward anyway, I would never allow anyone in again—ever.

I was a statue with a mechanically beating heart. When I finally came alive, I realized I was not a terrible daughter but a normal one. But God does not stop at normal. Ascending from the ground to discover and live your real purpose pulls you out of the "normal category." Running away from trial instead of sticking around, surrendering instead of fighting, and hating instead of loving it cages you there.

The spasm of this revelation jerked me out of numbness and false hope. The air was scented with the truth. I smell good now. I can move on. I don't have to live with the ghosts of my past that haunted me for years and covered me with shame. Those kinds of ghosts stink.

This spiritual side of the sense of smell is addressed in 2 Corinthians 2:14-15.

Thanks be to God who always leads us in triumph in Christ, and through us diffuses the fragrance of His knowledge in every place. For we are to God the fragrance of Christ among those who are being saved and among those who are perishing.

It is not only she that lived with it, but we watched her suffer, and we suffered with her. We waited and prayed. We hoped and groped, gave in, and gave up. I loved and hated and laughed and cried. I waited again, walked in, and walked out. I started, ended, and started over.

Dad would say, "That's life."

How many years languished while I, oblivious to Mom's magic, only saw her as a burden? When the self-condemning thoughts creep in, I replace the feelings of guilt with these four facts:

- She is sick and blind to it.

- The sickness masked her beauty, rendering it almost imperceivable.

- My shame and fear masked her beauty, rendering it almost unrecognizable.

- My shame and fear masked *my* beauty, rendering it almost incomprehensible.

When I separated her from the illness, I could release her from it and love her in and out of psychosis. This conquered my fear of her condition and its emitting symptoms and the ugly stigma attached to it because love conquers fear. I found an answer in 1 John 4:18 "There is no fear in love; but perfect love casts out fear."

Love conquers stigma because stigma comes from fear. The struggle was worth it. Overcoming my fears made me a better person. It made me love her mind and embrace her regardless of the circumstances.

She didn't change. I did.

I learned to love the difficult, different, and mundane. The hateful, haughty, hopeless, and helpless became easy to love because they are me. I learned to love myself. Dropping the guilt and shame, I was amazed at what I could finally see in me—real beauty. Learning to love her mind enabled me to love myself and others genuinely. I could finally turn toward her in love and see her as Christ sees her and me—loved. I became a better wife and mom. I could really love them without fear of not pleasing them or doing them wrong. As forgiveness set me free, I set them free to be who they are meant to be. They know I love them across galaxies. They believe me when I say, "I love you."

I cherish the times Mom somehow knows when I am sad even when I try to hide it. When in treatment, she has the capacity to be aware and sympathetic to my feelings and be interested in my life. She imparts sage advice on how to grow my flowers and frets when my teens venture off to faraway places. I had waited for my whole life for her. Eventually, I had stopped hoping she would return. But it's better than a miracle.

It's a mother and a daughter loving each other.

Notes

Chapter 4

1. FactZoo.com. "Tawny Frogmouth—No, It's Not an Owl or a Puppet." Last modified 2015, https://www.factzoo.com/birds/tawny-frogmouth-not-owl-not-puppet.html.

Chapter 9

1. Rebeccca Woolis, *When Someone You Love Has a Mental Illness: A Handbook for Family, Friends, and Caregivers,* New York: Penguin Putnam, 1992, 132.

2. Treatment Advocacy Center. "Ohio," 2018, https://www.treatmentadvocacycenter.org/browse-by-state/ohio.

Chapter 13

1. WebMD "What Causes Schizophrenia?" Last modified June 29, 2020, https://www.webmd.com/schizophrenia/what-causes-schizophrenia#1.

Chapter 14

1. Rick Warren, *The Purpose Driven Life: What on Earth Am I Here For?* Grand Rapids: Zondervan, 2012, 218.

2. Zondervan, *Daily Light on the Daily Path.* Grand Rapids: The Zondervan Corporation, 1981, 217.

Chapter 15

1. Apa.org. Lea Winerman, "The Mind's Mirror." October 2005, https://www.apa.org/monitor/oct05/mirror.

2. Loretta Bates (@lorettabates), "Have You Ever Heard of Mirror Neurons?" Instagram photo, June 12, 2019, https://www.instagram.com/p/BynKJeElRy5/.

Chapter 16

1. Howard Halpern, *How to Break Your Addiction to a Person,* New York: MJF Books, 1982, 8-9.

2. Halpern, *How to Break Your Addiction, 25.*

3. Halpern, *How to Break Your Addiction, 76.*

4. Halpern, *How to Break Your Addiction, 39.*

Chapter 17

1. A.J Russell, *God Calling*, Uhrichsville: Barbour Publishing, Inc., 1989, August 16.

2. Russell, *God Calling*, September 3.

3. Russell, *God Calling*, November 8.

Chapter 19

1. E. Fuller Torrey. "Schizophrenia is a Brain Disease," 2010, http://www.schizophrenia.com/disease.htm

Chapter 20

1. Russell, *God Calling*, March 20

2. Russell, *God Calling*, October 8

Chapter 23

1. American Psychiatric Association. *Diagnostic and Statistical Manual of Mental Disorders Fifth Edition DSM-5* (Arlington: American Psychiatric Association, 2013)

2. American Psychiatric Association. *Diagnostic and Statistical Manual of Mental Disorders Fifth Edition DSM-5* (Arlington: American Psychiatric Association, 2013), 101.

3. Xavier Amador, *I'm Not Sick, I Don't Need Help!* New York: Vida Press, 2010-2012, 46

4. Innovations in Clinical Neuroscience. Douglas Lehrer, "Anosognosia in Schizophrenia: Hidden in Plain Sight,"

2014, https://www.ncbi.nlm.nih.gov/pmc/articles/ PMC4140620/#B4.

Chapter 24

1. World Population Review. "Columbus, Ohio Population 2020", 2020, https://worldpopulationreview.com/us-cities/ columbus-oh-population.

Chapter 25

1. Mentalhelp.net. "Schizophrenia Symptoms, Patterns and Statistics and Patterns," 2020, https://www.mentalhelp. net/schizophrenia/statistics/.

2. Xavier Amador, *I'm Not Sick, I Don't Need Help!* New York: Vida Press, 2010-2012, 225-226

About the Author

Cecile Bibawy has a never-ending desire to spread the truth about mental illness, inspire people to tell their story, work toward ending the stigma that keeps people sick, and promote the health of mind, body, and spirit.

After sunrises and coffee, that is, when she's not writing, she's exploring the pursuit of truth, goodness, and beauty with her children as she and her husband classically homeschool them. She teaches Zumba classes and tells her stories and struggles to anyone who will listen. Bibawy was a public relations practitioner for

Faith Mission Homeless Shelters in Columbus, Ohio and also promoted Job Corps for a while in Upstate New York.

She is available for keynote speaking about her story to your people. Find Cecile at cecilebibawy.com, Facebook, Instagram (@sincerelycecile), on her front porch, and at her favorite coffee shops.

S.T.I.R.®

Speed up recovery · Talk about it · Instill hope · Remove stigma

Let's stir up love and life
for better mental health.

cb

CECILEBIBAWY.COM

CPSIA information can be obtained
at www.ICGtesting.com
Printed in the USA
LVHW100104070522
718057LV00002B/73

9 781647 464981